MW01227895

Living Shoreborn

A Glimpse into Life on the Eastern Shore of Virginia

Barry Mears

Edited by
Kamryn Mears

Contents

For my Shoreborn friends and family. This wouldn't be possible without you.

Chapter 1

Roots Run Deep

L et your mind paint the picture of a hunting and fishing paradise—bright blue skies with puffy white clouds hovering over golden fields of grain. The woodlands are alive with wide varieties of wildlife. You are only minutes away from the largest estuary in the United States, the Chesapeake Bay. The same is true if you are headed east. You will encounter the seaside creeks and marshes that lead to the barrier islands and ultimately the Atlantic Ocean. The sunsets are both breathtaking and inspiring. This utopia does exist. We call it the Eastern Shore. I am blessed to call it home.

I learned from a very young age that being Shoreborn would have its advantages. Once your toes have been filled with marsh mud, you will always remember the sensation. That distinct smell will serve as a reminder that you are once again home. Shore living is a slower pace.

Some may say we are fifty years behind the rest of the world. I would say that is a good thing. Our citizens are advocates for faith and family. Most of our small towns have at least one church and some others have two or three. We are a family here on the Eastern Shore, one of the last remaining communities where neighbors know one another and will stop what they are doing to help those in need.

As for my family, my father died when I was a small boy. My mother served both roles as she provided for my older sister and I. Mom was a nurse by trade. She knew the meaning of hard work. Like many others in her generation, this woman had no quitting spirit. This was one fearless lady. I remember many of her sacrifices and the long hours that she worked. Despite her busy schedule, Mom always made time for us kids. She inspired me to appreciate the outdoors. She would take my sister and I crabbing. Long summer days were spent on an old dock, attempting to lure a large jimmy crab with a chicken neck. Looking back, I realize how much my mother's efforts impacted my entire life. What a blessing it was to be raised by such a wonderful woman.

My first boating experience was with my Uncle Joe. We would cram five people onto an old wooden scow. The outboard motor would arrive at the dock when we did. Uncle Joe kept the 9.9 Seahorse in the trunk of his car. As a child, I used to think Folly Creek was a hundred miles long. Perhaps the two-hour trip to the Coast Guard station was due to the overcrowded boat and small engine.

During those times, I discovered my love for fishing. My mother would help me tie rigs. She imparted in me the most important virtue in fishing: patience. Mom was always a top-the-leader board in the fish count, and this still rings true. Summer days flew by in a flash under the blue sky and a refreshing coastal wind. We would fish for hours. When the low tide arrived, everyone got out of the boat. We would use rakes to dig clams on a sand bar to accompany the feast that we had previously harvested. Even as I clam today, those memories come to mind. Uncle Joe taught me various methods, including "signing." This was searching for visible indications that a clam was nearby. The sand would have a keyhole shape, suggesting that the tasty treat was just below the surface. When the rake touched the clam, it made a distinct sound that signified your efforts would be fruitful. All of these lessons and encounters helped me when I first ventured to the creek on my own. My first solo journey would take place when I was just fourteen years old. Now, you might be wondering how a 14-year-old boy travels to the creek and back home without a boat. That brings me back to my wonderful mother. Her shift at the nursing home was from 7 a.m. until 3 p.m. She would get up several hours early to transport me and the boat to the dock. Later that afternoon, she would pick me up after she finished her eight-hour shift at work. I spent many summer days alone on Folly Creek. I went clamming, walking the beaches, and fishing. A remarkable experience, especially at such a young age. I wasn't aware of it at the time, but I was developing a deep love and respect for our lovely and peaceful way of life. I can instantly transport myself back there in my mind whenever I hear a seagull laughing in the distance or come across an old cedar duck blind. Such a wonderful childhood for a Shoreborn boy. I wouldn't have wanted it any other way.

The beauty of the Shore is not limited to being on the water. As fall approaches, nature paints our wooded areas into a mosaic of vibrant hues. Autumn ushers in the harvest season and farmers shift into high gear. Before the weather turns cold, they must remove the crops from the fields. Jim Evans and the crew at Evan's Farms in Greenbush are ready for the task. Acres of grain are devoured by large combines. Wheat is the main winter crop, followed by corn and soybeans in the summer. Sportsmen begin to divide their time between the fall rockfish season and the start of the hunting season. This usually starts with a dove, goose, and duck. Larger game like whitetail deer follow soon after. Our wildlife is abundant. The tradition of hunting is as old as the Shore itself.

home serving as the main headquarters. One by one, the hogs made their final sacrifice. Meat began to fill large galvanized containers. My sister and I had the responsibility of getting the meat inside as members of the participating youth. The ladies would methodically chop the pork into the proper cuts. Ham, bacon, loin, shoulder, and pork chops. Not even the feet were wasted. Some of the men were loading up the head and sorting through the not-so-handsome insides. The intestine was cleaned and used as a sausage casing. Everything served a purpose.

This day taught me several lessons. Shore folks were tough, hardworking, and for the most part self-sustaining. These are images that will only live on in our minds. I will always treasure the amount of time I was able to spend with family. It saddens me to think that today's children will never experience these moments. Even though everyone has since passed away, their memories will live on in my Shoreborn mind.

Chapter 2

Slice of Heaven

Growing up on the Eastern Shore taught me a lot about the changing seasons. Not just in the literal sense of weather, but also in terms of life's seasons. In the spring of my adolescence, when I was still in my teens, a chance encounter would forever change my life. I was introduced to a young crabber by the name of Lee Wirth. His office was a crab shanty in a little bayside town called Deep Creek, making him easy to find. Lee taught me about the Peeler crab. Lee is a family man and an expert on crabbing, after all it is in his blood. If you remember, I had grown up on the seaside. There weren't many crab-shedding operations. My first encounter with the Chesapeake Bay was about to commence! In my old wooden scow, I bought my first dozen peeler crabs. Newman Scott Jr. always contended that Lee buried his money in mason jars. I can neither confirm or deny that claim. My knowledge of new waterways like Onancock and Pungoteague Creeks began to expand. The beauty was understated but breathtaking. The channels were wider, and the water was more clear than at the seaside. To my surprise, there weren't sandbars every few feet. I'd develop the habit of fishing off Parkers Island with my newfound bait. A peeler crab is to a large drum what a soft crab is to you and me: delicious!

The Crabhouse of Lee J. Wirth

The following few decades would be spent on the hunt for game fish like red and black drum and speckled trout. I felt most at ease bringing the boat up to a marshy island known as a "Tump." This is essentially a method of fishing in shallow water from the bank. If the crabs were fortunate enough to escape the fish that were on the prowl, they would take refuge in the eelgrass. The hard shell of the crabs was able to be shed; this is the process known as molting, which is crucial to a crab's growth.

As I became older and more adventurous, I ventured deeper into the bay and discovered Watts, an uninhabited island that was home to pine trees and sandy beaches. It wasn't until later that I discovered the island had formerly been occupied by both humans and animals. Once upon a time, a lighthouse illuminated the path for vessels traveling up the bay, but Watts Island has suffered as a result of erosion and storms, and it has been divided in two. As you sail along her banks, you'll notice stumps from once-thriving pine trees that are now submerged beneath several feet of water. Even today, you can walk along Watts' beaches and uncover Native American artifacts. It saddens me that a place treasured by so many generations will one day vanish beyond the Bay's horizon.

I plotted my course as being due west of Watts Island as I forced my bow into a two-foot chop. I could make out what appeared to be a small village's skyline off in the distance. Crossing the deeper water of Tangier Sound, a popular channel for large vessels, always appeared to get rougher. The water became smoother as I neared the shore. The term for this is "Slick Cam," as Lee Wirth had previously taught me. As I approached the first-day marker, I noticed a most welcoming sight: Port Isobel, a magnificent introduction to Tangier Island. I felt the same excitement as Captain John Smith must have felt when he first beheld her shores in 1608. My eyes were wide open while an entire city emerged from the water. Crab shanties and docks were connected together. Handcrafted work boats were moored to each Captain's dock, and crab pots were neatly stacked in rows. A beautiful location that I had only ever experienced through the vision of artist

Willie Crockett. His incredible paintings came to life in front of my eyes. Round sterns, box sterns and ducks flying over the marsh. A sight to behold for a young pair of Shoreborn eyes. As I idled through the harbor, I noticed that everyone took the time to wave and smile. I tied up my boat to a large dock that had a sign that read "Parks Marina." The dock where I first set foot on Tangier Island was where I overheard a loud voice saying, "She ain't cold none! I believe it will snow." Given that it was 95 degrees outside, I was a little confused. I soon came to appreciate Tangiermen's sarcasm and dry humor. Being raised on Tangier allows its people to maintain their distinctive and recognizable accent, which is one of its best attributes. A tradition that dates back as far as the island.

The man then said, "I didn't catch your name."

I asked him for his and told him mine.

"Mark Crockett, but everyone calls me Moony," he said.

He might have acquired the nickname since he was located closer to the moon than most. He was much taller than me—I'm around 6 feet. He started teaching me about the island's history. It was his "home," as he put it. Though we had only recently met, I soon realized that Moony and I shared a lot more in common. Love of the outdoors, water, our way of life, and the places we both called home. That was the first of many visits I would make to Tangier. I spent the remainder of the day exploring the island. Similar to Captain Moony, I came to the same conclusions after speaking with each resident: Tangier men and women are kind, hardworking, humorous, and deeply defined by their faith in God. "God's country" is a term you'll hear me use. Shining examples include Tangier and the Eastern Shore. God appears to have spent a little more time on our little slice of heaven. While navigating the narrow streets, I stumbled across a railway. There was a young man underneath a deadrise applying a new coat of bottom paint. He was working in tight quarters, and we appeared to be close in age, so I saw this as an opportunity to make a new friend. I introduced myself. With his brush still dripping in copper paint, He said "I'm Stewart Parks, but everyone calls me 'Stew Pot'." I assured him that I was pleased to make his acquaintance. At that point, I came to the realization that everyone on Tangier must have a nickname. Stew and I would remain friends for many years to come. He was one of the most genuine stand-up guys I've ever met, similar to my first bayside friend, Lee Wirth. I began to realize that many Eastern Shoremen shared the same enthusiasm for the Shore as I do. Unfortunately, Tangier is suffering terrible erosion; hopefully, this beautiful paradise can be saved. I will always treasure the memories of my first trip to Tangier, whether I go there in person or just in my mind.

After topping off with fuel, I wanted to explore more of the bay. I ventured just a bit north. Another small village, like Tangier, appeared on the horizon. On a misty bayside day, a big water tower was readily visible. I noticed that there were more boats in this harbor than at Tangier. I came to the realization that I had stumbled across Crisfield, Maryland, a picturesque bayside community established by Benjamin Sommers in 1663. In the past, Crisfield was known as Anniemessex, after a local Native American tribe. In 1866, an attorney named John W. Crisfield aimed to bring a railroad to the town. To recognize Mr. Crisfield's efforts, the town would go on to become officially incorporated in 1872. The town adopted his name, which was the primary reason for all the boat traffic. To get mail and other necessities to Tangier and Smith Islands, a lot of traffic moves through Crisfield. Many Island residents would travel to Crisfield for a day trip so they could shop in nearby Salisbury, Maryland, or in Pocomoke City. Like most towns along the Bay, Seafood is King, mostly hard crabs, and Crisfield still hosts the world's famous Crab Derby.

I moved toward Long Dock's main street, where I saw a man speaking into a microphone, as well as another man holding a large camera. I listened quietly as I walked up to him. With a strong shore accent and a slow southern drawl, he was able to weave a tapestry of Eastern Shore themes with his words. He seemed to be speaking to me directly; like a poet, he portrayed the sensation of a warm sunrise shining on one's shoulder or going fishing with family. He evoked with his words a sea breeze and a salty mist rising from a boat ride. He spoke with passion; this man was no actor; he was the real deal. He cherished the traditions of the great outdoors and the Eastern Shore. I realized I had just met the southern gentleman, Scorchy Tawes. He took the time to share several fishing and hunting stories with me, which I still remember today. What a blessing it was to have met Scorchy, they truly broke the mold with him. Not wanting to overstay my welcome, I returned to my boat to see what else was around the next salt marsh. In those days, the majority of people used a compass and a chart to navigate. I wasn't entirely sure where I was, but I was moving toward another small hamlet. Compared to my last two stops, there weren't as many houses around. Since there weren't many people around to ask for directions, I was delighted to see a man working diligently to scrub a nearly spotless crabbing boat. After all, cleaning one of those is challenging.

I idled up beside the man and asked him for his name.

He looked up at me and said, "Dize, Smitty Dize."

I then curiously asked him, "Smitty, exactly where am I?

"You're in Ewell, son," he chuckled.

He tried to clear things up by adding, "This is Ewell, around the corner is Tylerton, and over yonder is Rhodes Point!"

I couldn't have been more perplexed.

"Smith Island son, you're on Smith Island," he remarked with a grin.

In my mind, everything began to come together. Smith Island was another location visited by John Smith in the early 1600s. From a peak population of approximately 800 people, it now has over 200 fearless residents.

The people I met were like those I'd met in other places. Kind, diligent, and tough as nails. One thing I discovered in all of these towns was dedication to work. The people relied on their faith and fortitude to survive. I gave old Smitty a tip of the hat and threw my scow back into the wind. I needed to make one more stop before returning to Onancock.

I set the compass to the east coordinates of 90 degrees. The journey from Smith Island to Saxis took roughly around 40 minutes. This was another Bayside Island discovered by John Smith in 1608. Saxis, which has a fleet of Chesapeake Deadrises, is referred to as a seafood paradise. The workboats were put to the test by severe storms and catastrophic flooding. I've come to understand that nothing can stifle a Shoreborn soul's spirit. While bouncing around the White Caps of Pocomoke Sound, I saw two large flocks of Seagulls in the distance. A closer glance would show that the gulls were looking forward to a free meal. Captain Barry Johnson, also known as "Diddy Mouse," was getting ready for another soaking with his nets. Ronnie Denston was pulling his last row of crab pots aboard. The birds seemed to float in the bay breeze, chatting back and forth in search of finding a morsel of misplaced crab bait. I really couldn't tell who was more at home, the men, or the birds. As I got closer, my friends Marcie and Homer were waiting for me; they were busy at the Crab House fishing out soft crabs. I tied up next to their dock and saw a young girl splashing and having fun in a crab-emptied float.

"What a wonderful way to grow up," I thought to myself.

She was occupied with releasing starfish and seahorses to the Chesapeake Bay. I then noticed Carroll Lee Marshall sitting on an old wooden bench, a block of wood in one hand and a knife in the other. As a young man, I was astounded by how a person could transform an ordinary block of wood into a work of art.

Carroll gave some advice, saying, "Son, you just take a piece of wood and trim out everything that doesn't look like a duck!"

This was a humorous approach to teaching one about an art form that takes decades to perfect. Even today, Saxis Island remains one of my favorite locations to visit.

Ducks Unlimited Carver of the Year, Carroll Lee Marshall

It had been hours since I had eaten lunch, some left-over pizza from Pappy's. I was picturing how delicious a CherryJane cheeseburger would be. I had my compass set to 180 degrees due south. The sun was setting lower in the western sky. As I made my way closer to land, I went by some of my favorite fishing places, including Bernerds, Half Moon, and Guards Shore. White sandy beaches took on an orange hue. With the sun settling in below the horizon, my final destination for the day was Southside Chesconessex. I find the people on both sides of the creek to be equally charming, even though the Northside is where my grandmother grew up. I had my sights set on Schooner Bay when I rounded Tobacco Island. That meant I would arrive in time to stop by Johnny Taylor's store and buy a Coke and some peanuts before he closed. A lively day on the Chesapeake Bay ended in friendships and experiences that will last a lifetime. That salt air will put you to sleep like a baby. And sleep I did.

Vintage Eastern Shore Round Stern

Chapter 3

Burt - A Chesapeake "Tail"

I remember the first time I stumbled on a quaint little village called Quinby. With my old scow behind me, I stopped by a house with a one-word advertisement that simply read *"BAIT"*. This turned out to be my first meeting with Rudolph and Phyllis Powell. They were like characters from a book, doing a terrific job of portraying a hard-working Eastern Shore family. Phyllis led me out to the back in an old shed, where there was a massive tank full of live bull minnows and two large freezers stuffed to the brim with squid and silver sides. Rudolph, a soft-spoken man, was shucking clams over in the corner. I realize that, like my grandfather, the Powell family did not see this as a hobby but rather as a means of their survival. This amazing couple taught me so much. They played a major role in why I grew to care so much about our citizens over the years. Mind you, nothing fancy, just a family of faith, hard work, and an honest way of life. The small seaside village named Quinby, Virginia, will always hold a special place in my heart.

Spending time alone in the outdoors is for the birds. I realized I needed a companion, and that's when fate intervened, and I received a phone call from my old pal Mike Gentry. He couldn't wait to show me the latest member of his family. I fell in love with this block-headed, ball of fur with a small white spot on his chin. His coat was curly and shiny, and he appeared to have just left a beauty parlor. He was the runt of a litter of Chesapeake Bay Retrievers.

I then said to Mike, "That's exactly what I'm searching for, a pup just like him."

Much to my delight, Mike responded, "If you want him, you can have him!"

I graciously accepted, unaware that I had just met my best friend and that a 16-year adventure would unfold right before our eyes. The first thing I had to do was give the little fellow a name. I noticed that he had a way of bearing his teeth that gave the impression that he was smirking.

I said, "You think you're cute, don't you? You look like Burt Reynolds."

Although "Burt" was not the usual name for a Chessie, he wore it well. We would go on to spend a number of wonderful moments together.

In the early days, Burt was too little to jump from the dock into the boat. He had salt water coursing through his veins. Regardless of the water's temperature, he would always jump in with his tiny puppy legs. Anyone who has ever worked with a retriever of any breed is familiar with the Golden Rule: patience. Burt was as stubborn as he was intelligent, so I had to devise a technique of training him because I could not wear him out by tossing a ball or even a retrieving dummy. I used to hit golf balls onto our field from distances of 100 yards, 200 yards, and occasionally even further. He galloped like a racehorse to recover each ball, dropping them at my feet with pride. I told you he was smart! Burt would always bring me my old golf clubs because he knew where I kept them. Every afternoon we played a round. He was better at golf than I was. I can still picture Burt and I traveling to Willis Wharf in the early spring. Off Cobbs Island, the drum fishing was outstanding. We enjoyed that town because it had four stores: Annie Doughty's, Will Johnson's, Jim Hamlin's, and Ballard Brothers. There, you might find any tasty treat a young man and his puppy could desire. His coat shimmered in the morning sun. Many a soul would tell me how handsome he was. I thanked them and thought, You try living with him. The true fact was I couldn't have parted with him for a king's treasure. There is a certain bond between a man and his dog. The love between us was a given, without uttering a single bark.

Cobb Island was a long boat ride from the dock. On the bow, Burt had his own space. He reserved the right to bark at everything he saw, including seagulls, dipper ducks, and the occasional day marker. My work had only begun when we arrived at the beach; rods, coolers, and gear would be transported to the ocean. Burt, on the other hand, was in his element with sandy dunes and endless beaches to frolic in all day. There were strict rules regarding where you could go walking during piping plover nesting season. Being that I could walk directly from the creekside to the beach, I had no trouble abiding by the guidelines. I was unaware that I was about to learn a costly lesson: a piping plover egg and a golf ball have a striking resemblance. By this time, I had set up my surf rods and was eagerly awaiting a bite. I spotted a man in a uniform approaching my area. I wasn't concerned because I've always taken satisfaction in fishing and hunting within the limits of the law. In the hopes that his visit wouldn't last too long, I started to gather my credentials.

His tone quickly changed from irritated to furious. Then, with a raised voice, he asked, "Do you mind explaining this?"

Before I could make a defense, he was standing next to my cooler, and to my surprise, there were roughly a dozen piping plover eggs inside. When Burt arrived, he dropped another one at my feet in the same manner I had taught him on the driving range. The conservation officer was not amused, and neither was I when I saw the total of the fine that he had given me. This was only one of many challenges Burt and I would overcome. Chesapeake's can occasionally be onry and temperamental over the years, but the one thing that seemed to ease Burt's soul was his view from the bow of an old scow. He wasn't just a fair-weather dog. I recall going to Wachapreague around dawn on a snowy morning with Burt. An Eastern Shore duck hunter is a distinct breed, similar to a Chesapeake retriever. The experience seemed to be enhanced by the frigid temps and cutting winds. Anyone with common sense would have turned around and gone home to sit by the fire, but Burt and I had each other, and that was enough. I cracked a path through the ice in front of us by using an old wooden oar to break it. Burt proceeded to bark and flash his trademark grin when he heard the old seahorse startup. I remember how cold those days could be; after all, an old cedar-branch blind didn't provide much protection from Mother Nature. That didn't matter much to a young Shoreborn boy and his dog. That day, mallards and black ducks were flying along with the occasional teal. If you shot quickly enough, you might just get dinner. Burt was dancing in the blind with excitement, and I spent the majority of the morning scolding him to settle down. He was waiting for one thing: an opportunity to do what he was born to do: retrieve. A pair of blacks dipped in low for a look. I jumped from my seat to try and bag a double. I shot once with success, the second shot, well, you gotta be quick. It was time—I gave Burt the command: "Retrieve." I pointed him in the direction, and he took care of the rest. He would flawlessly swim out to the target, then methodically make his way back to the blind. I can't say he did it on purpose, but he used to take great delight in shaking off his curly brown coat and covering me in salt water and mud. After all, it was in both of our veins. Wearing a little bit of marsh mud and salt water is like wearing a badge of honor. As much as Burt and I enjoyed our winters, we looked forward to springtime. We patiently waited for warmer days at a small store in Greenbush owned and operated by Truman Lewis. Most towns had some sort of General Store, and many of them served double duty as the local post office. These old wooden structures with creaky plank floors had their own charm. Most of us will recall the sights and smells for a lifetime. A large wooden barrel full of pickles sat in the corner. The counter was stocked with pickled eggs and pickled pigs feet for those brave enough to eat them. I was more of a cloth bologna and cheese boy myself. In those days, loose change had value. For less than a dollar, you can get a sandwich with a cold Coca-Cola and have enough left over for a pack of peanuts to go in your soda. Even a penny was valuable. There was a rack with an assortment of candy: Mary Janes, Squirrel Nuts, and Hot Balls. All for the price of one cent. Those days, like mom-and-pop stores, are long gone. They were the good old days when towns could sustain themselves. My grandmother used to send me to Trumans to pick up the groceries. I'd run into my Pop there, who was purchasing a bag of bolts. To this day, I can still smell the wheel cheese.

One of Burt's and my favorite past times was riding around in my old F-100 pickup. She had a six under her hood and a three on the tree gear shift. You wouldn't have to worry about that being stolen nowadays. The kids wouldn't even be able to drive it. Burt loved to stand in the back and bark at everything, from butterflies to bumble bees. Anyone that has ever dealt with a Chesapeake retriever knows how spirited they can be. I remember one afternoon we had ventured down to Hacks Neck. This was a remote bayside town. Hacks Neck has a rich history, just like the majority of these villages. The folks are like most towns: friendly, strong, and proud. I loved my rides down that neck with Burt. Before it got dark, we figured we would have time to ride down to Harborton dock. I knew it was getting late when the street light came on over Greg Smith's crab house. I wanted to let Burt out for a run. There was only one problem.

A gentleman and his wife were at the dock, admiring their brand-new boat. They had their beautiful chocolate lab with them. Burt was a good dog and a great companion, but he felt he was the tall hog at the trough. He didn't play nicely and didn't like other dogs. When I put him in the cab of the old Ford, he was about to go crazy trying to confront the other pup. As I began to pet the other lab, he appeared to become a bit more agitated. The couple was prepared to launch their brand-new Scout, a beautiful new fiberglass boat. Burt's loud barking and whining seemed to be holding the woman's attention. I assured her that she was safe and made a promise not to let him out of the truck until they had placed their boat in the water, a promise I kept—

Almost.

As they idled away from the ramp, I figured it was safe

to release my hound. How could I have known that this guy would hug the dock as he became familiar with his new controls? Burt ran down the dock at full speed while I screamed at the man and his wife to pull away. When he finally got the message and started the boat, I quickly covered my eyes as a 120-pound Chesapeake Bay Retriever was flying through the air. As you could imagine, he landed in the middle of that man's brand-new boat. Burt introduced himself to the lab, but the two dogs did not get along. I was about to lose my voice yelling at Burt as the woman was crying and screaming, the man was cursing, and the boat was rocking and rolling. I told the guy to "just throw him overboard," and eventually he used a life jacket to subdue the attacker with a swift snatch of the collar. Burt was still in the water, making a fool of both himself and me. He swam to shore, knowing I was upset, and hung his head while I tried my best to apologize to the stunned couple. That was the last time I saw those folks. They must not have been too angry since they both gave me a thumbs-up as I left the creek.

At the Onancock Wharf, Old Burt had a big fan club; the fishermen loved playing with him and trading stories around the Liar's bench. Willie Crockett nicknamed him "blockhead," but I'm not sure if it was because of the shape of his head or his reluctance to learn and listen. Winter Cullen, Colbourne Dize, and Mac Rogers are a few of the men who enjoyed throwing the ball for Burt. I would use the babysitting opportunity to go to Freddy's barbershop and get a haircut. Frank Hartman was always there talking about shooting pool. His son Jerry and grandson Jimmy were among the customers. Ole Freddy was quick and efficient, and the experience always made me think of Floyd's Barbershop on The Andy Griffith Show; I guess it was a small-town feeling. On my way back down to the dock, I'd stop at Wise's drug store, which served the best tuna sandwich I had ever had. I'd wash it down with an ice-cold Sprite. The rest of my time was spent chitchatting with some of my old friends. Back then, Onancock was a wonderful American town for a small child, much like Mayberry, where everyone knew each other.

It was getting late by this point, and I had wasted enough time uptown. As I made my way down to the dock, I found Burt sleeping on the floor of Winter Cullens' boat, "The Soybean." Late in the afternoon, when anglers like Andy Dize and BW James were just getting off work, the dock would become very busy, and the drum bite was hot. I loaded ole Burt up in the back of the truck. My mother had asked me to bring home a few items from the store. Fresh pride was the new name for what was once Acme market. I pulled up in the parking lot. I admonished Burt to stay in the truck and assured him I would be back quickly. This store was a little fancier, with an automatic door to let you in. I was about finished making my way up and down the aisle when I heard a bloodcurdling scream. My initial thought was a robbery. I knelt down and inched closer to the noise as shouting and cursing added to the commotion. The only weapon at hand was a jar of pickles. Peaking around the corner, I couldn't believe my eyes. That's where I first saw the intruder, a giant brown fuzzy ball named Burt. He had followed me into the supermarket and entered through the automatic doors. He made his way to the back of the store and found the meat counter, where he was helping himself to a big fat steak. What a commotion he caused; the staff were scared to death. Then, I was reminded of the expensive fine from the piping plover eggs.

I created a plan and, leaping into action, screamed, "Get back, that's a stray dog!"

As I got closer, a woman cried out, "Stay away from him, Mister; he'll take your head off!"

I assured her that I was an expert on such matters. Burt was as stubborn as he was mischievous, but he wasn't dumb. My request for him to "kennel up" was the one command he obeyed every time. This was his order to get in the truck or be left behind. I screamed the command twice, and he hurried for the door. I followed closely behind and promised the store employees that I would see to it that the vicious beast was removed from the grounds. In the truck, we both went. Needless to say, Mom did not get her groceries that night.

Chapter 4

Rite of Passage

W hen we were teenagers getting our driver's licenses and first cars, we had a ritual of driving from Four Corner Plaza down to Fork's Grill and then to the Onancock Wharf. On that loop alone, I probably put 100,000 miles on my old truck. Like most teenagers, getting into some mischief was never out of the question. Long before we had earned the right, my friends and I enjoyed a few adult beverages. One of us had the dubious task of getting the hooch every Friday. One Friday in particular, it was my turn to make the score; I heard that Robert Cobb's store had the coldest beer around. I decided to make the purchase myself; some might call it a rite of passage, while others would call me crazy. They warned me that he was a police officer, and I sat in the parking lot for a half hour working up the courage to go inside. While practicing my deep voice in the rearview mirror, I noticed that I was shaking a bit. As I entered, I tipped my cap to Mr. Cobb and made my way to the back of the beer cooler, where two frosty six-packs had my and my pals' names written all over them. I made my way slowly to the counter. I figured I'd grab a newspaper as all the old guys did. As I set the items on the counter, I felt him staring at me. There was a long pause and I was unable to breathe. "Busted," I thought. Slowly, his hands moved toward the cash register, and Mr. Cobb blurted out my total in a gruff voice. I gathered myself and handed him the money. When I came outside, my friends were stunned; they greeted me like a folk hero. The beer was put on ice, and we all went home to prepare for the weekend. The party would always start in front of the Acme Market. Some had beaters, while others had hot rods. Chevelles, Camaros, and GTOs. We'd spend a couple of hours shooting the breeze. Around 10:00 p.m., we would start the cruise into Onancock. On my third trip, I saw what no driver ever wants to see: blue lights. From a fun evening blasting Creedence Clearwater Revival to now facing the police, we knew we were in deep trouble. I eased to the side of the road, where I couldn't see much. My eyes were filled with bright lights, and the officer ordered us to exit the vehicle in an agitated voice. It was at that point that I realized the man was none other than Robert Cobb. He lectured us about our speed and loud music. They weren't major crimes, but underage drinking was a different matter altogether. He made us put our cooler on the hood of his patrol car.

He had my license in his hand, glaring at it through the beam of his flashlight.

"Son, says here you are 16 years old, is that right?" he asked.

I answered quietly, "Yes, sir."

I could tell by the look on his face that he knew he had us dead to rights.

His next words were, "Do you mind telling me where a young punk like you got beer?

Being in enough trouble, I figured I'd better tell the truth.

I said softly, "I bought it from you, sir, earlier this afternoon down at your store."

I saw a blank expression on his face as he walked slowly back to his car and loaded up the cooler.

He looked over his shoulder and shouted "You boys get the hell out of Onancock, and I don't want to see you anymore tonight." I think the outcome of this situation would be different today.

When Chrome Bumpers were a thing

Onancock has a unique history of its own. Today, the town is known as a quaint waterfront destination with shopping, boating, and fine dining. In fact, Onancock's first claim to fame was as one of King James' original royal ports. Onancock, Virginia was chartered in 1680, known as Port Scarborough, despite the fact that the hamlet's history dates back far more. The 1700s were tumultuous times on the Chesapeake Bay. British warships were on the lookout for any vessel that was asserting American sovereignty. The Declaration of Independence, signed in 1776, did not dispel the animosity between the two countries. In the 1780s, the battles were still ongoing. The tides started to turn in 1781, the date of Cornwallis' surrender in Yorktown. This historic event prompted Commodore Zedechiah Whaley to sail up Onancock Creek to meet with Lt. Colonel John Cropper. Whaley asked for help on his flagship, The Protector. Cropper gathered two dozen of his men to assist Whaley in forcing the British out of the Bay. The crew was vastly outnumbered, and many of Cropper's men perished in the battles. It wasn't until 1784, when the Treaty of Paris was enacted, that tensions between the two countries began to subside. The newfound peace was welcomed and Onancock was set to explode with new economic opportunities. The first accomplishment was a stagecoach route that stopped in town. This was the first efficient method of connecting passengers and light cargo to the port. Warships were being converted into cargo vessels. When the Hopkins brothers set up shop at the wharf in 1842, they quickly grew into the largest commodity trading facility on the Eastern Shore. Wagons packed with Eastern Shore produce flocked to the growing town. Ships were loaded, and goods were transported to cities such as Baltimore and Virginia Beach. By the time the railroad arrived, Onancock had earned the reputation of being Virginia's busiest port. Onancock's history is an excellent conversation starter—A wonderful topic the next time you're enjoying a cup of coffee at the Foggy Place.

Onancock "Old Timers Day" in the 1960s

Chapter 5

Barnyard Magician

I spent many of my days hanging out with my grandfather. Pop had a unique way of connecting with animals. Ralph Melson was known as the "Original Horse Whisperer" on the Eastern Shore. His stables were always filled with horses, goats, chickens, and other critters. He was not the typical farmhand. His livestock were actors, and he was their trainer. Pop worked with these animals for countless hours, molding them into the farmland showmen. As part of the show, goats were trained to walk a tightrope, and ponies were taught to ride a bicycle. I loved watching him work with the animals. It was an all day process except the 2pm break so we could listen to Swap Shop. This was a popular radio program on WESR. Charlie Russell would take phone calls from folks with anything to buy, sell or trade. I liked it when Kelley hosted. Her voice was much more melodic and she typed much faster than Charlie. Butch had a velvet voice as well. We never missed an episode. Pop's reputation was well- known. Paul Merritt was a gentleman from Chincoteague Island. Mr. Merritt operated what could be considered a museum on the island, complete with pony rides and shows put on by Pop. Big names were no stranger to my grandfather. Misty of Chincoteague, a famous Palomino, was the subject of a popular book by Marguerite Henry that was later adapted into a film. Pop knew Misty long before she found fame and fortune because she had been through his training program. Phantom Wings and Wisp O' Mist, two of Misty's offspring who were once a part of the Melson Farm and had quite a pedigree. Riding with him to Chincoteague to work with ponies was a highlight of my youth. He taught me the real meaning of patience and perseverance. He methodically worked with each animal until they would respond to simple voice commands - That's a trick I'd like to teach some people. Part of the show had Pop dressed in a western outfit, he would sing a song while the pony trotted in a circle. When he said "bang," the animal lay lifeless on the ground. He would tug on the reins, begging the pony to rise. The well-trained animal would stay motionless until the performance reached its climax. He would yell, "There's no saving my horse, bring me a spade," as he hyped up the crowd. That was the ponies' command to jump up and trot again, or suffer the fate of being buried on the site. I never knew how he was capable of communicating with animals. They loved him, and the audience did too. To me, he was purely a legend, and most importantly, my Pop.

Step right up! The show is about to start! - Ralph Melson working his magic as one of the Eastern Shore's greatest Showmen

A journey to Chincoteague is a treat for any Shore-born boy or girl. When I was a youngster, just the trip across the causeway was able to capture my imagination.

Every pond was filled with that distinct marsh mud smell, oysters sticking up on the low tide, and ducks and geese. Anyone who has ever developed a love for the shore marshes would certainly call this place a paradise. Fish houses were a full operation back then, but the island was mainly recognized for its nearly century-old tradition of pony penning. Tourism was slowly claiming more of the tiny Islands' real estate. As for me and Pop, we had different business on the tump. We'd visit his good friend Delbert Daisy. His nickname was "cigar," which he earned after a run-in with a game warden many years ago. Cigar was a nice old man, and his shop was filled with old wood-working tools and wooden blocks. I would wade through a pile of wood chips as he and my grandfather talked. Ducks were spread all over the floor. Some finished, but mostly just bodies and heads scattered about. I was unaware of it at the time, but this was my first encounter with the legendary Eastern Shore carver, "Cigar Daisy." Mr. Daisy would go on to inspire my lifelong infatuation with wooden decoys. Cigar would lean back in an old wooden chair, holding my full attention as he told me stories from years ago. Early in the century, waterfowl was a huge industry on the island. Northern markets were paying top dollar for ducks and geese. Money was tight during war times, and duck hunting became an occupation for both the honest and the outlaws. Large shotguns were assembled to kill as many ducks as possible; these weapons were bulky and heavy, earning the name "punt guns." Ammunition for these guns ranged from nails to glass. Trapping was another popular method for harvesting the quackers. There are many stories about how Cigar earned his nickname; he contended that he only lost a few cigars while trying to retrieve some ducks from his trap. Some speculate that there is a lot more to the story. He said that the Game Warden recognized them as his brand, and that day "Cigar Daisy" was born. Carving decoys became a tradition and an honest way to earn a living. Carvers like Doug Jester, Ira Hudson, Miles Hancock, and Cigar were in high demand. As the sport of duck hunting gained popularity, hunters would buy these wooden birds to use while hunting. These decoys were usually sold in a group called a string of six or more. These old wooden decoys had been beaten up in the bottom of Chincoteague scows and were peppered with lead shot. While some were hollow or had keels installed, others were weighted. That became the carver's style. These masterpieces evolved into a kind of folk art over the years. Decoys became more of a collector's object as plastic replaced wood as a more practical hunting tool. The list of popular carvers is large; if you think this is a business of chump change, you would be wrong. One of the birds that cigar had carved for his wife was valued at a tidy sum of $150,000. Today, the market determines the cost of wood carvings. If someone is looking for a particular bird to complete their collection, the sky is the limit on how much they are willing to pay. You can bet that more people are buying them than are selling them. Once you own a Miles Hancock or an Ira Hudson, you will understand. The nostalgia, history, and craftsmanship can never be duplicated. This is a tradition I'm glad to say is still alive to this day. The sons and grandchildren of some of these greats are using similar methods to create a treasure that you and I can place on a mantle to honor those days gone by.

My Pop and I would travel from Chincoteague and end up in the small seaside village of Greenbackville. This is a small fishing community located across the bay from Chincoteague, a boomtown 100 years ago. Franklin City was located on the town's east side. The Worcester Railroad was extended from Snow Hill, Maryland to Franklin City. In 1876, the shores of Chincoteague Bay were the end of the line for the railroad. This offered Waterman a much more effective way to market their perishable products. Franklin City was a crucial part of Eastern Shore history. Once a bustling hub of commerce and prosperity, now a ghost town. Salt bushes have claimed the railroad tracks, and the memories have faded into a Seaside Horizon. We were there on modern affairs. Pop loved hearing the fishing report from his friend Perry Romig, a friendly fellow who always offered a smile and a good tale to tell. These stories captured my imagination, and it was there that I met Bill Mariner and J.T. Bolding, who both always had a story to tell about their adventures on the high seas. I was blessed in my youth to share the deck with the Shores' most accomplished fishermen.

One thing remained a fact: If you were looking for a good time on the Eastern Shore, you were more likely to end up in a Seaside or Bayside town. One of my favorite stops was Bayford, a quiet bayside community on Nassawadox Creek. Many lazy summer days passed by under a Shoreborn Sky. Bayford had something for everyone, including fishing, crabbing, and swimming, to name a few. It was a safe and fun place for young people to gather and live during the best moments in their lives. I remember a long line of Boston Whalers tied up at the dock. Everyone did business with a gentleman who became somewhat of a local legend. He had a name that fit his title - Hooksie! He was a kind man with a genuine love for people. He had many roles, such as postmaster and shopkeeper. He spent his entire life in Bayford, enjoying farming and working on the water. He was a World War II veteran. I remember him as a walking encyclopedia on everything related to the Chesapeake Bay. Hooksie was known as the mayor of Bayford, and many locals got their first credit line from his store. Most likely spent on a cold Coca-Cola and a wild bear sandwich.

Family-friendly events were abundant in the good old days on the Eastern Shore. Tasley's A&N Speedway was one of these outings. This half-mile dirt track was an enjoyable and exciting experience. Race car drivers such as David Fowler, Ronnie Denston, Lewis Earl Lilliston, and others would trade paint on this short track, much to the delight of their fans. These drivers achieved folk hero status. Each week, a legion of loyal fans would come out to cheer on their favorite drivers. It may be Johnny Gardner in victory lane this week in his 1955 Chevy - that is if he could get around Bobby Thornes, Larry Hamlin, Earl Annis, and the rest of the field. These teams were made up of friends and family, and the drivers worked on their own cars. From dirt track racing to big trucks competing in mud hops, racing has always been in the blood of Eastern Shoremen. Sponsors help teams with some of the funds needed for competition, rather than corporate sponsors as you might think of them today. Family-owned businesses like C.A. Lofland, Coffman Fishers, and Country Magic Restaurant, just to name a few.

Fun days at A&N Speedway were the norm back then. After a long day at the track, everyone was looking forward to the opening of Onancock Carnival. The loyal members of the Onancock Fire Company organized this magnificent event. Many memories were made on this hallowed ground. I remember the excitement I felt as a boy. When we rounded the corner, the black spider and the bright lights of the Ferris wheel glistened against the background of a dusk evening sky. The place was always busy. Before you even stepped foot on the property, you were greeted by the most pleasant of aromas; funnel cakes were awaiting a fresh splash of powdered sugar, a line was already forming at the french fry stand, and hamburgers and clam fritters sizzled on a flat top grill. I was busy eying some cotton candy. After all, the carnival was the only place to get such a treat. I can still picture the small train that navigated its way around the grounds. The conductor blew his whistle to alert everyone about the arrival. Vintage carousel horses followed each other in a perfect circle. What better name for an attraction than a merry-go-round? This ride was located in the center of the grounds, and a nice Pavilion was built over it. In the distance, you could hear Jack Truitt working his magic at the "Chuck O Luck" game. "Three sixes, three sixes, that's a triple six!" he would shout. If luck were on your side, a simple quarter could net you a cool $1.75 by the end of the evening. Each booth had something different to offer. Perhaps you were in the market for a stuffed animal; just put your change on the lucky number and spin the wheel. I remember my grandmother repeatedly trying to win a cake. This was a great place for making new friends and reconnecting with old ones. We felt a sense of freedom when we were kids. We got to walk around the carnival grounds unsupervised. Many first dates were taken to the carnival. Most likely the place lovers held hands and perhaps shared a peck on the cheek at the very top of the Ferris wheel.

Youngster's favorite pastime was playing baseball for the Little League. The field was located directly behind the Onancock Carnival grounds. When the smell of the grill filled the air, it was hard for a young slugger to concentrate. Getting into the carnival early meant you didn't have to stand in line for tickets. That snow cone stand was always popular; there was something very poetic about shaved ice coming out of a stainless steel machine on a blistering hot Shoreborn evening. Choosing which flavor to add was the hardest decision we had to make at that time. I remember how safe we all felt at the carnival. There were always Accomack County deputies present, in addition to the fire and EMT personnel. Penny Parks seemed to hold everything together in the office. When she was in charge, everything was smooth sailing. Lazy summer nights would blow away with the breeze. Eastern Shore folks enjoyed a fun evening with not a care in the world. Most of us never missed a night when they were open. The event was so popular that the Roseland Theater closed because all of its patrons were attending the carnival.

The Onancock carnival rewarded everyone for their loyalty. The climax of the occasion, decades-long Fourth of July firework displays, brought shore folk from near and far. This Independence Day celebration was revered as one of the best on the Eastern Shore. It offered a great viewing spot. The vibrant colors, the bombs bursting in the air, and the loud booms thrilled both young and old. I remember sitting in the back of an old pickup truck thinking this was the greatest show I'd ever seen. After all, we had a united and patriotic feeling, which is something that most small towns in America value. I will always cherish my nights at our beloved and long-gone Carnival. Of course, Onancock wasn't the only show in town. Wachapreague also put together an incredible event. The one clear difference was that familiar marsh scent, which has endeared so many to our little slice of heaven. In between the squeals and laughter, stars shone in the Seaside sky, and in the distance, one could hear the surf of the Atlantic.

Chapter 6

Good Ole Seasiders

Nestled on the Eastern side of the Shore, Wachapreague has a rich history and unique story. For centuries, Wachapreague has been chronicled for its outstanding hunting and fishing. In the early days, a busy port attracted many people searching for their fortune on the high seas. The Native Americans were the first to enjoy her bounty. Wachapreague translates to "Little City by the Sea." Nathaniel Bradford, one of the first settlers, received a patent for the area in 1662. John Teagle's family was the first group of Europeans who settled in the region. John Finney bought the land from Teagle in the 1820s. A few years later, Finney sold the Powell Brothers a portion of the land, and they chose to change the name of the village from Wachapreague to "Powellton". There was a lot of confusion surrounding the new name, and it would only last for a brief time. Eventually, everyone came to an agreement, and Wachapreague became well-known as a waterfowl paradise all up and down the east coast.

Prominent politicians, the rich, and the famous were among those in search of adventure far from the city. A sprawling Hotel Wachapregaue welcomed guests with open arms. There was a hunting clubhouse for those outdoorsmen to enjoy. Vintage boats that local craftsmen had handcrafted filled the harbor. Wachapreague was a dream come true for anyone who loved fishing, hunting, relaxing, and enjoying the Shoreborn way of life. In those days, "gunning" was a big business Much like Chincoteague, many of the local's livelihoods were dependent on it. Young men earned their living as hunting guides and charter boat captains. This is a proud tradition that will follow for years in the little city by the sea. Captains like Ray Parker would emerge as living legends in the modern era. Captain Ray braved the ocean blue with many different vessels, including the Betty Lou, Skilligalee, Ellen Raydean, Evelyn Cree, SeaBird I, Skipper II, and SeaBird II, as well as his prized Whiticar, the HOBO.

Captain Ray Parker aboard the legendary "HOBO".

Decades of experience made the old salt a master of his craft. Charter boat fishing seemed to be in the blood of the Parker family. Ray's brother, Captain Earl Parker skippered the Virnanjo. The vessel was named after Earl's wife, Virginia, and his two daughters, Nancy and Joann. These wooden boats were works of art. Like snowflakes, there were no two the same. Many of these workhorses were built close by in Quinby by Bill Welch and Archie

Doughty. Many generations of anglers enjoyed adventures off the coast of Wachapreague. Offshore fishing has never been for the faint of heart. The day starts early, Like 2 am early. When going on a journey 60 or 70 miles off the beach, you need an early start. The Captain was always the first to arrive at the dock. Saltwater is his lifeblood and he needs it to survive. The half-sleeping crew shows up shortly after. Once all the gear is loaded a Shoreborn adventure soon follows. The roar of the engines and diesel smoke fills the pre-dawn sky. The weather on the Atlantic Ocean is not always kind. When you're living depends upon this income, you learn to deal with it.

Shortly after the fleet leaves the dock, radio chatter starts on the way to the inlet. Captain Jimmy Wallace on the "Canyon Lady" would be heard calling for Sam Parker on the Scorpio. Both captains were waiting for BW James to chiming in aboard the "James Gang." The men would compare notes and try to agree on a hotspot where they could drop the lines. Once arriving at the inlet, the calm seas of the creek were long gone. The inlet was difficult to navigate due to sandbars and breakers. Once plowing past the first bell buoy, the mates' work on deck had only just begun. For some, mating was a summer job, while for others it was a family tradition. Young men like V.J. Bell were busy tying Ballyhoo and separating flats of butterfish. The fishermen would take in the scenery, and some would start nibbling on a sub sandwich they had purchased from Margaret Carpenter's store the day

before. The smell would draw you in while picking up
some last minute tackle from Bob Fate. The Fleet would
stay pretty close together until each Captain plotted his
own course. Carey Dean Roberts was Capt. on the BOZO
II. On the port side was Claude Webb, captain of the Sea
Robin. Gordon Eastlake in the Margo A and Tommy
Colonna in the Sallie Lee were not far behind. Nat
Atkinson in the "Foxy Lady" were off the starboard side.
He was trailing behind Bobby Turner in the Bonnie Sue
and Zed Lewis in the Pathfinder. Captain Gene Crockett
was in the lead aboard the Main Squeeze. The waves
seemed to dance under the stars as the tip of the sun
pierced its way over the horizon. It had already been a
good day, and we were just getting started. The time had
finally come to put some bait overboard. The JMAR set
cedar plugs off the stern. The lures darted back and forth
in the churning white water; These were the flat lines
closest to the boat. The idea was to attract a big fat tuna to
the surface. Off in the distance, you could see a green
machine skipping across the seas. The anticipation of a
bite is in the mind of every angler on the deck. There is no
better sound than a screaming drag and a rod bent double.
The tight line plays a tune like a banjo in the ocean
breeze. Meanwhile aboard the "HOBO", the action was
just getting ready to heat up. The first sign of a prized
white marlin is his bill piercing the ocean's surface.
Veteran mates like V. J. Bell live for this moment. Marlin
can be as finicky as an old cat. The bait teases the fish as
he smacks it around deciding if it is a meal. The biggest

tease is to the angler on deck. V. J. went to work to hook the prized game fish. Using years of experience and expertise, the mate started stripping line from a Penn International in an effort to keep the big fish interested. The next few minutes were tense. Capt. Ray screamed the two most important words in all of fishing: "HOOKED UP!" Eager angler Butch Belote was handed the rod and the show began. More like an acrobat than a fish, the frustrated game showed his displeasure with jumps, back flips, and an occasional summersault. With each crank on the reel, the marlin is getting closer. These sharp billed monsters are exciting to catch. They are not much for table fare . Most are released to fight another day. The HOBO and the rest of the Wachapreague fleet had a tradition of flying flags . These flags represented each species of fish in the ocean. Without bragging or uttering a single word, folks could see the success of each crew as they returned to the safety of Wachapreague Harbor. The members of the crew would gather at the Island House for a great meal and a few well-deserved beverages. Many days the winds and waves would not permit off shore trips. That is where Wachapreague earned the title, " Flounder Capital of the World."

The tiny seaside village has been a popular destination for anglers in search of the tasty bottom dwellers. I remember folks from up north always called them "fluke". One doesn't need a 40-foot Viking to go flounder fishing. These fish can often be found sunning themselves on a shallow flat where the water is a few degrees warmer. For those just looking for a day trip, experts like Capt. Nat Atkinson and his son and 1st mate, Jared could be chartered to put you on the action. Not everyone is cut out to be a flounder fisherman. These sight feeders can get lockjaw as fast as any fish in the sea. My mother seemed to be able to figure out the flatties on most fishing trips. More often than not ole Babs caught the most and the largest. I suppose that's how she earned the nickname "Flounder Whisperer". When it comes to enjoying the harvest at the supper table. There is no better meal than fried or broiled flounder, served with cornbread and some fresh spring garden asparagus. My mouth is watering a bit as I think about it. Just another great benefit of Shore living, God's Country. Some anglers don't need a fancy boat or a giant tackle box to target their fish. The Surf fisherman is a different breed entirely. The journey to get to that perfect spot on the beach is a mission in itself. Carts with large rubber tires were loaded with everything needed for the day. Beer, bait, and tackle were dragged as much as a mile down the beach. Old pros like J.T. Bolding and Bill Mariner knew all the best haunts to hook up with a salty sea monster. Different seasons bring a variety of trophy fish looking for a free meal in the churning white waters of the breakers. Early spring would kick off with the first black drum run. Bull red drum and monster striped bass soon followed. There are fishing tournaments up and down the east coast where these anglers compete for prize money and more importantly bragging rights. Veteran surf fishermen like George Phillips, Bob Hutchinson, and Joe

Sparrow joined forces with J.T. and Bill to form the Eastern Shore's own team. The name was: *"THE EASTERN SHORE OF VIRGINIA ANGLER'S CLUB SURF FISHING TEAM."* Master anglers like Kenny Ainsworth, Bill Hall, Chuck Bradford, and Allen Evans were brought on board to add to the talented group. This core group earned many trophies and that is no fish tale. With dominant performances in multiple tournaments, the team quickly earned the reputation of the " best in the business." Over time, the coveted spots on the team would be held by a whole new generation of expert hand liners. When top hooker Jamie Logan joined the team, he revamped the name to include "FISH HOGGS". A name they certainly earned over the years. Marty Bull, Brian Hill, Clark Crockett, Danny Kidd, and Ray Willett along with Ray's son, Ethan serving as an alternate rounded out the team. Decades of experience and tradition are on full display every time the team stepped foot on a sandy beach. Dominating most of the tournaments they entered. The Fish Hoggs have represented the Eastern Shore with pride and excellence. After all, who would bet against a bunch of Shoreborn fishermen?

Chapter 7

Backs On or Off?

Not everyone goes to the beach in search of a fish tale. The Eastern Shore has some of the most picturesque shorelines. The sandy beaches and vast marshes offer a perfect habitat for all kinds of wildlife. For those folks into beach combing, the treasures are abundant. There is something very calming about the sound of waves lapping on the shore. Many people can spend the entire day in search of peace and tranquillity. Millions of seashells and sand dollars glisten in the mid-day sun. Many artists and carvers walk the beaches looking for the perfect piece of driftwood. Long before Europeans arrived, Native Americans depended on fertile land and water for their survival. Native artifacts, mostly arrowheads and stone tools, can still be found thousands of years after their original inhabitants. These were the only part of an arrow that was able to survive the test of time.

The shaft was crafted out of tree branches, and the fletching was done with all-natural turkey and hawk feathers. Depending on the area, stones like Jasper, Chert, Flint, and Quartz were shaped into razor-sharp points for hunting. When I visit some of the more secluded locations, I wonder how long it has been since another human being set foot there.

Some beaches on the Eastern Shore don't have regular visitors. It is easy to get away from a crowd of people by discovering your own private spot. Some people prefer the beach towns' party atmosphere. There are numerous options available in this area. Kiptopeke and Cape Charles, located on the southern end of the Shore, offer beautiful views and shallow water that is safe for children to swim. For years, packing a cooler and going to the beach has been a weekend pass time for Shore residents. Just two examples include Cedar Island and Assateague. Ocean City Maryland is a short drive away for those looking for more action. Like most places near the water, this beach town has a rich history. The Algonquian tribe of Native Americans was the first to live there, and they enjoyed great fishing from her Shores. English-born Thomas Fenwick once owned the majority of the land that Ocean City was built on. Businessman Isaac Coffin constructed the first beach cottage to be rented in 1869. The rest is history. Later, in 1875, the Atlantic Hotel could accommodate 400 guests. This marked the beginning of Ocean City's transformation from a small fishing village to a popular resort destination; visitors came from all over the world. The first boards laid parallel to the shore were welcomed at the turn of the century. As businesses flocked to the thriving town, the iconic Boardwalk expanded from a few feet to nearly three miles. Many smiling children have been amused by the century-old Trimper's amusement rides. There are plenty of games, food, and beverages, and many iconic names have been associated with the town. Dolle's popcorn and Thrasher's french fries had been reason enough for some families to load up the car and travel for miles just to enjoy the familiar treats.

Ocean City has something for everyone, from the very young to the most seasoned among us. The most popular activity on and around the boardwalk has remained exactly the same for over a century. I'm not talking about Volleyball either. I'm talking about people-watching, a tried-and-true pastime. As the generations change, so do the styles and fashions. You can sit on a bench for hours without losing interest in the sights. A smile is one trait that the majority of visitors share. Many of the game attendants take on the role of modern-day Carnival Barkers; Taunting bypassers chanting "Step right up ladies and gentlemen!" This was an effort to grab your attention by encouraging the family to compete for a stuffed animal. I could probably retire if I could recover every dollar I spent on attempting to win Dumbo. In the daylight hours, the beach is lined with thousands of sunbathers. The oceanfront was full of jet skis and power boats. From a bird's-eye view of the resort, thrill seekers are lifted hundreds of feet in the air over the water. Soaring just above them, small airplanes fly banners advertising the best deal on pizza and a bushel of crabs. As the fishing boats come and go throughout the day, the water in the inlet never stops churning.

From a small fishing village, Ocean City now hosts the White Marlin Open, the most lucrative and prestigious tournament on the entire east coast. This event attracts fishermen from all over the world, including basketball legend Michael Jordan. It's no secret that folks visit our neck of the woods in search of sand, salt, and sun. You don't have to be Shoreborn to know that Delmarva is known around the world for its abundance of fresh seafood. We have the Atlantic Ocean and the Chesapeake bay in our backyard. The Blue Crab is one of the most popular items on the menu; these tasty creatures live in a perfect environment and reside on all sides of the Eastern Shore. The male of the species is known as " Jimmy," and the females are known as "Sooks." Crab potting is the most common method of catching these hard crabs. Baited pots are thrown overboard in the hopes that some wayward travelers will stop by for a free meal. Most fishermen check the pots daily. The little ones return to the water as the adults are harvested. Trot lining was a method used in the early days of crab harvesting, in which a weighted line was submerged with an attached bait on display every few feet. As the boat moves forward, the watermen skilfully raise the line to the surface. With the aid of a dip net, each crab that is hanging on the bait is retrieved and placed into a basket - A very labor intensive process. Some traditional-ists continue to follow this method. In the past, dredging was used to harvest crabs during the winter. This was a practice that implored scraping the muddy bottom and scooping up the dormant crabs. Modern regulations outlawed this harvesting method. The Eastern Shore hard crab season starts in March. Veteran watermen like Joe Stalgaitis, Donnie Kilmon, and Ricky Parks set out their pots in the creeks by the sea. This is usually the first spot the bottom crawlers emerge from their murky winter abode. Early in the season, captures may be scarce. In an industry built on supply and demand, the price of a scarce commodity can go sky-high. For the die-hard crab lover, there is no premium too high. In the early spring, a bushel of crabs can easily cost $200 to $300. Restaurants and patrons wait in line to get their hands on the first run of crabs. There will be disagreements about how to clean, serve, and eat a blue crab. I guarantee that any baysider or seasider you ask will gladly share their thoughts on the topic. It all begins with a single question: *"Backs On"* or *"Backs Off?"*

'Tis the season!

For those unfamiliar, crabs are steamed alive in a large pot. Some claim that leaving the hardshell on the crab during cooking helps seal in the flavor, while others say it is significantly less work. The people on the other side of the issue say that the little extra work pays off. These chefs remove the hard shell just before steaming A simple garden hose is used to flush out all the " dead men" and "mustard". This method offers far less mess at the table and allows the seasoning to penetrate the entire crab. No matter where you stand on the debate, I think we can all agree that we love steamed crabs. However, The controversy does not end there There's also the age-old dispute over the perfect seafood seasoning, which will require a bit of a Shoreborn history lesson.

The story starts half a world away in Germany.

Gustav Brunn, a young spice maker, was busy perfecting new recipes. Most of Mr. Brunn's seasonings were used in sausage. He started to enjoy some success when circumstances changed his fate. Early in the 20th century, tensions in Europe grew, forcing Gustav and his family to immigrate to the United States. Gustav Brunn landed on the Shores of Baltimore, Maryland. He quickly set up shop and returned to doing what he loved. In those days, there weren't that many sausage makers in the United States. That didn't deter Gustav from working on his spices. Locals discovered another use for Brunn spices. In 1940, he perfected his concoction, which would go on to fame, fortune, and the seafood industry. You may have heard of it, perhaps you have used it Gustav named it "Old Bay" after the waters that greeted him to his new home. This tongue-tingler is my go-to condiment for everything from french fries to chicken wings. If you believe that the Great Spice Debate has been put to rest, hold onto your hat. A gentleman by the name of Stringle might be in disagreement. Shortly after Gustav and his family arrived, Mr. James Ozzle Stringle and his wife Dorothy moved from the small island village of Tangier to the large city of Baltimore. James, a waterman by trade, was also very familiar with seafood. Many people will claim that Stringle is responsible for the best seafood seasoning ever invented. Shortly after Old Bay gained popularity, his recipe was perfected on Pratt Street in Baltimore. The name, J.O. Seasoning, was named by none other than Mr. James himself. When comparing the two, people will make a hard line in the sand. I believe I can bring us back together with some vinegar, melted butter, and an ice cold beverage.

Seafood has a way of bringing people together in a festive manner. The industry of harvesting salty treats has changed dramatically over the years. Tiny canoes have been replaced by giant vessels. These crews venture out into the Atlantic Ocean from Chincoteague Island. Sometimes the trip lasts as long as a week. They are in search of solid gold treasures like scallops, chonch, and fish. The variety of species in the Delmarva region makes us a major player in the global seafood market. Some watermen are after one creature in particular, not for its delicious flavor, but for a far greater reason. Scientists conduct important studies using the unique blue blood that flows through the veins of the horseshoe crab. This discovery has led to many medical advancements to help people. Unlike the tasty blue crab, which pays the ultimate price for satisfying our tastebuds, the horseshoe crab is only bothered long enough to extract a bit of blood. After that, they are safely returned to their natural environment. A true marvel of nature. These modern boats have the best equipment. Electronic navigation and hydraulic tools have alleviated some of the grueling labor of the past. It goes without saying that I had to add the "Arster" when talking about popular seafood on the Eastern Shore. If you have never heard of this, you are probably just pronouncing it wrong. President George H.W. Bush once penned a letter home while he was stationed on Chincoteague in the 1940s. He wrote about his new love for the salty seaside oyster. In his writings, he joked about how the locals referred to them as "Arsters" and the harvesters as "Arstermen." Whatever you call them, they are one of the most sought-after meals in our area. The oysters flourish in both the Chesapeake Bay and the seaside creeks on the ocean side. The methods of retrieving them date back centuries. One practice that is still alive and well today consists of a hammer, a basket, and a hearty soul in a pair of hip boots. The young oysters, known as spats, attach themselves to structures like rocks. The skilled oystermen use their hammer to gently tap on the adult oyster, breaking the bond while keeping its framework intact. These creatures act as giant filters, another marvel of nature. They naturally remove impurities from the water. Naturally, this method of harvesting must be accomplished in shallow water. Most of the time, the activity is planned around the low tide cycle; however, when that cycle moves west, the baysiders do it a bit differently. On the Chesapeake Bay, the oyster boats vary in size. One thing they all have in common is a crab dredge on deck, which is attached to a cable on a reel. Once the dredge has been lowered to the bottom, the skilled Captains will drag it for a distance. When the time is right, a hydraulic lever is held to bring the heavy dredge back to the hoist. When the catch returns to the boat, the contents are emptied onto the culling board and the crew begins sorting through the catch. Anything other than a legal oyster is thrown overboard; this process is repeated until the legal limit of oysters is reached. This is a stark difference from those in the profession hundreds of years back.

Oystering on the Chesapeake Bay in the 1800s was not only back-breaking labor but also extremely dangerous. A new style boat was crafted just for the purpose of harvesting oysters. These modern-day warriors, known as Skipjacks, were built for a purpose. The sides were low to the water, making it easier to bring goods onboard. The deck was wide open to store the payload, a large pile of bayside oysters. The engine under the hood did not exist at the time, so the vessel's propulsion came from her sails and a little help from Mother Nature. That may raise the question, "How do you go about retrieving an oyster from the bottom in fifteen feet of water?" The answer was simple: there were tongs on deck. They had 20-foot-long handles and sharp metal teeth on each edge. A single soul would manually lower the device until it reached the bottom. The waterman would use a scissor-like motion to try to dislodge as many oysters as he could. Once full, the hundred-pound load was brought to the surface foot by foot. The next time you feel like you have had a hard day at work, consider what life must have been like hundreds of years ago on the Eastern Shore.

Even today, when you ride to the water's edge, you can see signs of days gone by. In some creeks, nothing but storm-beaten pilings and crab shacks are left. These areas were once thriving families who labored on the water, typically following in the footsteps of their fathers and grandfathers. Earning a living this way required dedication and sacrifice. When I ride down to some of the dead-end roads, I am reminded of so many Eastern Shore memories. Some see a twisted dock with boards missing. The wood that is there is slowly decaying into obscurity. Some of these shanties' windows and doors have been missing for a very long time. Mother Nature continues her relentless pursuit of these old structures. In my mind, I can hear people laughing and joking inside the shack and smell fresh seafood nearing a brand-new dock. I listen while seagulls chat above to express their approval as the engines wind down after a hard day's work. The crew is stacking the baskets to be taken inside and sorted. With my eyes still shut, I can see the children splashing in the shallow water. They were playing in a paradise, one that they probably didn't learn to appreciate until it was gone. Working on the waters is a family affair. There is no other profession that is more adversely affected by bad weather, tides seasons, and regulations. It takes input from everyone to be successful. Bayside and Seaside alike were home to these workhorses. It just depends on what neck of the woods you are from. Back in the day, Pete West and Bonnie Miles were often seen shedding crabs on Nassawadox Creek. Crabber David Brunk, a native of Maryland, and his family followed in their footsteps by establishing their own shedding operation. Up the bay a bit further, Charse Angle, Henry Parks, and Sam Brimer were harvesting softies in Harborton on the mighty Pungoteague Creek. Like Jack Hutchinson before him,

AL Pruitt was the boss at the nearby Hacksneck, where Nandua Seafood was established. Obadiah Sample and Frank Bennett were mainly in charge of the picking house. Remember that our seafood has been enjoyed all over the world. In the glory days of crabbing and oystering, hundreds of businesses were thriving up and down the shore.

Down at Morley's Wharf, Burton Charnock was hard at work. Meanwhile, George Spence set up his headquarters on the shores of the Machipongo river. Mr. Spence enjoyed the best of both worlds. His business, located on the Quinby bridge, was accessible by land or sea. This enabled Spence to purchase fresh seafood from local crabbers and oystermen, and not many items are fresher than a bushel of Harry Martin hard crabs. Mr. Martin sold many of his harvests to Mr. Spence, a popular seafood guru. That is the very essence of Eastern Shore living—from the salty waters to the trunk of an old Plymouth. The Bayside village of Deep Creek is just a little further up the road. Back in the good old days, there was more happening there than crabbing and fishing. Jack Johnson had a thriving oyster shucking business, the creek was alive with activity, and there was so much camaraderie that they often helped one another finish the day's work. Jack shared the creek with Tommy Johnson, Bump Savage, and Charles "Scotty" Scott. Sadly, these men are no longer with us, but they have left a legacy of commitment to their precious Shoreborn heritage. These men were able to hand down their knowledge to up-and-coming generations. Newman Scott Sr., the son of Scotty Scott, was able to make a livelihood on the water by relying on his experience with his father. There was no doubt that this was not a career for the wealthy. It was, however, hard, honest work with the satisfaction of keeping a tradition alive. Newman Sr. and his wife Sharon worked diligently to build their own soft crab business, and they instilled these values in their sons, Newman Scott Jr. and Michael. I am proud to say that these families are the best friends anyone could ask for.

If there were such a thing as a "favorite creek"—and I have navigated the Eastern Shore's waters from North to South, East to West—the choice would be clear. Because my grandmother was raised in downtown North Side Checonessex, this will always be my favorite place to soak a dozen peelers. There is a clear view of a weather beaten crab shack no matter which side of the creek you travel to. Each year, Mother Nature's winter wrath grows stronger. On Chessconessex Creek, the first sign of spring is a fresh coat of bright red paint on Lee and Bev Wirth's crab shanty. Along with that hard work comes the rebuilding of docks and crab floats, as the relentless winds and tides show no mercy to any man-made structures. The spirit the Wirth family has to preserve their way of life is one thing that never changes on the docks of this oasis. I've said many times that this is a family business, and the name of their workboat, "Four Sons," serves as proof of that. The Wirth family's four sons, Daniel, Nicholas, Adam, and Marshall, have been the heartbeat behind the family's crab-shedding operation. These young men were able to grow up acquiring values such as work ethic, dedication, humility, and faith. The time spent with their parents is another benefit that they will hold dear for a lifetime.

Chapter 8

Me and the Boys

Growing up on the Shore used to be like living in a fairy tale; no one felt the need to lock their doors, and windows were left open to welcome the summer breeze. We cherish many of these memories for one reason: when you're a child, everyone you love is present in your life. The reality of losing loved ones is an unfortunate part of growing up. The family unit has always been strong on the Eastern Shore; we didn't have the distractions that the modern generation does. On summer mornings in Greenbush, we were up with the sun. We lived by two golden rules in those days: First, get out of the house and play outside. The second rule is to return by dark in time for supper; the time in between would provide experiences that would prepare our generation for a career as an adult. The journey away from the homestead was usually taken on a bicycle, as this was the only way to find your pals back then. There were no cell phones; they were fastened to the wall at home, and there were much more efficient ways to communicate. The dozen or so abandoned bicycles in the churchyard were the telltale sign of everyone's whereabouts. As the boys and girls formed their teams for the football, basketball, and baseball games, everyone laughed and participated in the experience. Our parents felt safe enough to allow us to figure out things on our own. Looking back, I'm quite sure my mother would cringe about some of our activities.

My pals, Mike, Scotty, William and I loved to venture back in the woods for fun adventures. Perhaps it was there that I first learned to appreciate the natural beauty that surrounded our neck of the woods. As young boys, our main focus was building forts, and we each carried a pocket knife. The sole purpose of such a tool was to whittle down a stick or perhaps clean underneath our fingernails after digging up some earthworms. We would hang out in the fort until boredom took over. The pocket knife was not the only crude weapon we had. Each of us had a nicely tuned sling shot, with old pop bottles as our primary target. We knew the afternoon train came through town around 3:15 p.m. You could set your watch by that long lonesome whistle; how I wish I could hear it once more. Each of us had a pocket full of loose change, which we usually invested at Truman Lewis' store. On a hot summer day, a bottle of chilled soda pop filled with peanuts hit the spot. Some days, the coins served an entirely different purpose. There isn't a Shoreborn kid alive who hasn't thrown some change on the rail road tracks. I'm not sure what endeared us to this activity more —the excitement of a new souvenir or the fact that we didn't yet understand the value of money. The sound of the whistle became more faint as the train rambled down the tracks. The boys and I would count all of the railcars as they passed by. Our main focus was on one in particular: the last one! When the caboose was clear and all was quiet it was time to retrieve our prize. The massive weight of the train would smash the currency into a razor thin show piece. Certainly not the best use of money, but looking back, those memories are priceless.

It was not quite 4pm, we had many hours of daylight left to play. We all gathered in the churchyard and mounted on our bikes; Drummond's Mill Pond was only a 20-minute pedal away. Some kids liked to swim, so the gang jumped into the murky waters with no lifeguard in sight. Snakes, turtles, and lily pads joined in the fun, but that activity didn't last long. On the banks of the historic mill pond, I accomplished my best work. My Pop had crafted a fishing pole out of bamboo, and there was no danger of a backlash because the crude device lacked a reel. Like a page out of Huck Finn, I had a pole some string, and a hook. Bait, however, was not a problem. A fat night crawler or a noisy cricket seemed to work just fine. The thrill of catching a fish ages with the angler. Seeing a red and white bobber going under the surface is as exciting as hooking a monster Blue Marlin for a nine-year-old kid.

The banks of the pond had all types of creatures crawling around. We were either very brave or simply too naive to realize that playing with snakes is not a good idea. I can still hear the shrill screams of the girls as William chased them down the road holding a 6-foot black snake. I suppose enough time has gone for me to admit that not all of the crying came from the girls. We had no idea at the time that we were living the happiest days of our life. Our youth meant simpler times; we were innovators, producing our own source of entertainment.

It was quickly discovered that a simple baseball card could transform an average bicycle into a speed bike. The card was strategically placed between the frame and the spokes. The faster you pedal, the louder the rumble of your new Harley will be. We undoubtedly destroyed several costly rookie cards on the back roads of Greenbush and Parksley. The girls and boys made Jaxon's their first stop while in town; they have everything under the sun. We used to make a beeline toward the candy and toys, buying as many balsa wood gliders as we could. When times were good, we purchased the ones with a propeller. They had a little bit more range because they were assisted by a rubber band engine. Later, after a few base-balls and matchboxes, we were on our way. No kid in my day would be foolish enough to spend all of their money in one spot. The Lunch Box was our next destination; although they served the greatest burgers and fried chicken, we had our hearts set on something much sweeter. Martin Bull had mastered the art of preparing the perfect milkshake. My pals and I patiently waited for the Shirt Factory crowd to clear so that we could place the order; it was the best case of brain freeze I'd ever had. That was the only mind-altering substance back then. With our baskets full of cool trinkets, the short pedal back to Greenbush was underway.

Stopping by Byrd's Food to grab a couple of tomatoes for my grandmother was a common occurrence. In those days, we didn't need phones to communicate because everyone knew that the churchyard steps served as the headquarters for all the young people. We may have become separated over the day, but everyone eventually returned to the home base. After all, the afternoon air show was about to begin. Each glider was launched from the top step while the judges measured the distance on the ground during a best-of-three flying competition. The winner received a gourmet meal paid for by the not-so-sore losers, which typically consisted of a cloth bologna sandwich and a grape Nehi.

The sun was well on the west side of the Eastern Shore. As dusk approached so did our thirst for adventure. The older kids loved to tell the smaller children about the three haunted houses on the outskirts of town. The bicycles were mounted, and we rode to the old "Back Eighty Farm" after reassuring them that they had nothing to be afraid of. The old houses were spooky, to say the least. The windows were gone, and tattered curtains danced ghostly in the wind. We prodded each other until someone agreed to take the first step inside; the old boards creaked and moaned with each step, and there were exposed nails and broken glass everywhere. It's a miracle none of us got injured. The abandoned property was frequently exited in haste due to the sound of a slamming door. I don't believe in ghosts, but I have outgrown the desire to investigate. This a clear reminder that the spirit of adventure is alive and well during the innocence and naivety of our youth.

Not every day was spent in and around town. A visit to Mema and Uncle Joe's, who lived in a two-story farmhouse in Accomac, was a special treat for my sister and me. I loved hearing my grandfather and Uncle Joe share stories about life on the Eastern Shore. They both had perspectives on living through two world wars and the Great Depression. Their generation held a great appreciation for things many of us take for granted. When they were children, basic necessities like food and running water were not always readily available. They were largely self-sufficient and stronger as a result. They didn't waste anything and planned ahead for difficult times. Mema had the most beautiful garden I've ever seen; there wasn't a vegetable she couldn't grow. My sister Valerie and I would help gather string beans, peas, and butter beans. Once inside, the work had only just begun. Large bowls were placed on the counter, and we began shelling some of the delectable treats with the speed of a Ninja. My mom and Mema would process trash bags full of vegetables. Many were relished with homestyle meals, while others were canned for use during the bitter cold winter months. The pantry was my favorite area in the house, with shelves lining the walls and jars of sweetness filling each, including jellies, jams, and my personal favorite, fig preserves. We stayed busy and were rewarded with a sleepover; this was an adventure in and of itself, especially in the winter-time. Back then, a lot of homes used wood stoves to heat the first floor. When money is scarce, wood is a resource that can be gathered with a little muscle. The upstairs didn't have the same luxury; the registers were kept covered during the day to keep the heat downstairs. Early in the evening, they would open the ceiling vents to provide some heat into the upstairs sleeping area. My sister and I slept on a bed with at least a dozen layers of blankets. I remember snuggling under the covers and laughing about how we could see our breath. Looking back, that was the best night's sleep I'd ever had.

We woke up early, along with the sun. We knew that after the chores had been done, a new adventure awaited. Summer days were hot and muggy, even in the early morning hours. I can still picture myself running outside to retrieve the freshly laid eggs; that part was fun. Navigating around a sleep-deprived rooster, not so much. Some tomatoes had grown ripe enough to be harvested in the dawn sunlight, the songbirds whistled a tune, and everyone had a smile on their face. I never heard my folks complain about money, which makes sense given that we had everything we needed—and more.

Chapter 9

Family - Aunts, Uncles, and Cousins

When it came to feeling safe, Accomac was much like any other community on the Eastern Shore. We were trusted to ride our bicycles down to the drugstore for an ice-cold soda pop; this was a gathering spot for old timers to solve the world's problems. Another favorite hangout was across the street at Billy Payne's Texaco; he ran a full-service filling station. Billy would check the oil while he filled the gas tank, so there was no need for the driver to get out. With the occasional set of windshield wipers, you were on your way. Locals ran a tab and paid it off at the end of the month. This was a great time to be alive; everyone trusted each other and shared a mutual respect. I was at Payne's Texaco on much less official business. He kept candies, cakes,, and crackers in his office. Billy also had the hottest atomic fireballs west of

Piggen that all the kids craved. I can still remember how they made my eyes water. Billy was more than just a local businessman; he was family. He was wed to Nancy, Mema's daughter. Brenda and Deborah, the couple's daughters, were all part of a large family that could enjoy this lifestyle. In those days, no matter where we went, everyone knew each other or, at the very least, knew each other's people. There was another place that the kids liked to meet in Accomac. There was always something fun to be had around the old sawmill. Huge piles of sawdust covered the barns, and we loved diving into it from the loft, performing backflips and summersaults among other fancy moves. There was always some inherent danger in our activities, but it never seemed to slow us down. After a few hours of playing, everyone became hungry.

There was a sweet aroma blowing across town in a gentle Virginia Breeze. Scoby Duck had his smoker fired up with pork butts, ribs, and briskets. G. L. Smith and his wife Pat are well-known for their delicious barbecue. They perfected their sauce, the Accomac Blend, and the rest is history—Scoby Duck's Chuckwagon was born. To our delight, the boys from the neighborhood and I were able to taste test the smokey sensations. The smell even drew the attention of Ole Hoss, an interesting character we encountered every time we visited Accomac. He was always wearing a flowered blouse and smoking a cigarette, and his bicycle was as unique as he was — a giant steering wheel replaced the handlebars, and he had lights and an air horn. His attention to detail was impressive; he even had chrome mud flaps on his makeshift Peterbilt. As children, we assumed Hoss was rich. He was clad with jewelry. He had a ring on each finger and a large gold earring, which was quite a sight for a bunch of ten-year-old boys and girls. One of the rings on his left hand bore the Masonic emblem. When asked if he was a Mason, Hoss replied, "Hell no son! "I'm a Davenport, Jimmy Davenport."

This man would go on to earn the status of an Eastern Shore icon, with many funny stories about Jimmy and his misadventures. He once accompanied Lynwood Bundick on a trip to Florida on the semi. Legend has it that an argument broke out on the trip back home. Ole Hoss was told to get out of the truck and was abandoned on the side of the road near the Florida-Georgia line. Lynwood was always known for making good time, and his next stop was his home in Accomac. As the weary truck driver eased past the Court House, he had to slow down for a second look- you guessed it, Jimmy Davenport was coming out of the drug store with a cold Coca-Cola. He tipped his cap at Lynwood and said, "What took you so long, Hoss?" The Shore is blessed to have these great characters living among us.

The town of Accomac has a rich history. The Accawmacke Indians named Accomack County, which translates as "The Other Shore." One of the first eight counties in Virginia, Accomack County was founded in 1634 in the Virginia colony. The first jail, known as the Debtor's

Prison, was built in 1783. The 18th-century structure still stands today. The courthouse and other municipal facilities were built around the small jail. Accomac is also the birthplace of Henry A. Wise, the Governor of Virginia from 1856 to 1860. I remember getting my hair cut at Al Brock's barber shop, which was popular among the town's men for shaves and haircuts. These men told many stories about history from their own perspectives. Many of Mr. Brock's patrons were quite seasoned, with some being in their 70s and many more being in their 80s or almost 90s. They shared experiences about the old hotel as well as other local businesses. Time is forever changing the perspectives of those who lived it; these men were World War I soldiers. I can remember listening very intently as stories were passed along from the Civil War era on the Eastern Shore. These old men had fathers and grandfathers who had served during that time period. That is a history lesson you feel down to the core of your soul. I will always have the utmost respect and admiration for those brave souls. Not every story shared at the barbershop was so serious; I saw firsthand that men are significantly more efficient at gossiping than women. Even if the subject was a tall tale or two, the men would tease one another mercilessly and then all laugh together. This is small-town America, and I'm sure each of you can recall a place like this in your hometown. It was getting late, and I needed to get back to Mema's place. I paid Mr.Brock his usual fee of 50 cents for the trim. On my way out, I saw C. Boy, Joe, and Butch Lewis coming in for a trim. When I overheard them discussing an encounter with a grizzly bear while out cruising timber, I was fairly certain that a few more tall tales were about to be told. With one more bike ride around the block by Accomac Primary School, Val and I headed back. We stopped long enough to speak with Tommy Hines and Jack Lavelle. Like I said, everyone knows your name; it's all part of the Shoreborn charm in a place we call home.

We returned to find Uncle Joe exactly where we had left him. This trip to the garden netted nearly a bushel basket of carrots. We packed our things and gave everyone a hug and a kiss to hold them over until the next visit. We returned to Greenbush, but we would soon have more visiting to do, as was customary in those days. People came to visit, enjoy each other's company, and break bread together, a tradition that I fear is long gone.

A Match Made in Heaven - Ralph and Ora Melson on the Northside Chesconessex Dock

I remember going to the post office with my grandmother; there were always cards and letters mailed between friends and family from near and far. Sara Jane Mears, my father's mother, lived on 140 Market Street in Onancock and was often referred to as "Mama Sara" by the entire family. She told us of simpler times in town back in the 1930s and 1940s. When it came to money, things were always tight. People had something more valuable than money: they had each other. If one neighbor had an abundance of items such as chicken and eggs, they might be traded for meats and produce. The barter system was alive and well on the Shore. Many doctors received a side of beef as payment for delivering a baby. Mama Sara and I spent countless hours on her front porch, she liked to tell these stories, and I was an eager listener. She showed me where the milk bottles were left when Nelson Farms delivered door to door, and she recalled as a child seeing automobiles and horse-drawn carriages sharing the road. She used to tell me that I was born 100 years too late since I was enamored with historical stories. Thinking about it now, I'd say that her assessment was spot on — I wouldn't trade those memories for anything. Sadly, as time goes on, your memories become all you have. Loved ones leave us and new babies bless our lives; the cycle of life. Thanksgiving is one holiday that comes to mind; as a boy, I was able to spend time with my grandparents, aunts and uncles, and families who had traveled long distances to visit. As I've gotten older, I've grown to appreciate this holiday even more. Many souls have passed since my first Thanksgiving, and my role has changed as well. From a small boy crying over the thought of eating a turnip green to the position I now play as Husband, Dad, and PopPop. Time marches forward and we must embrace the change.

Chapter 10

A Christmas to Remember

I t all started with a magic marker and a Sears Roebuck catalog. The Christmas edition was called the "Wish Book", and many hours were spent turning the pages and making wishes. We were well aware that Santa Claus had a lot on his plate. Mother instructed us to circle a few of our favorite toys, and these suggestions would be passed on to the North Pole for consideration. I'm not sure if it was excitement or greed that got the better of us while we were marking the pages. Mine looked more like a Vince Lombardi playbook with the Packers trailing by ten points in the fourth quarter. My mother was rather baffled by the cross-outs, revisions, footnotes, and check marks. Christmas is usually a time of great excitement, and the Eastern Shore was a wonderful place for celebrating the birth of Christ. In the good old days, each town and business put up the nicest decorations. Shortly after Thanksgiving, every town would begin the process of stringing lights on the poles. Candy canes, bells, and Christmas trees were illuminated, much to the delight of young and old alike. A family ride in the evening from Cape Charles to Salisbury would get everyone in the holiday spirit. In the business district of most towns, stores line the main road. Those store fronts were meticulously adorned with items that would catch the attention of a young boy or girl. Many a parent nearly lost an arm to an eager youngster pointing out a new train set. Perhaps it was the beautiful bride doll that caught the eye; there wasn't a kid who hadn't worked their parents over for a bright red Radio Flyer wagon.

"After all, Mom, this isn't a toy; it's more of a tool, and I can help you around the house."

Two dolls on Christmas morning - Barbara Mears loving her 1960s Bride Doll

Walking into Western Auto in Exmore, I remember seeing a toy display like no other: doll houses, dresses, and

Easy Bake Ovens. There were bows and arrows and plastic survival knives with compasses in the handle; if you were looking for a toy paradise, this came close. My grandmother loved to shop at Glick's in Onancock; it wasn't my favorite store at the time because I was afraid of being double-crossed with some new socks and underwear as a gift. We would travel to Salisbury and visit what is now known as the old mall. As a child, this was considered a big adventure because there were dozens of stores lined with shining glass, and the fountains were loud as the crystal clear water fell back into the pool. Many people have thrown some of their fortunes into the water in exchange for a wish. This was the place I first encountered Chris Cringle, though, he wasn't the real Santa Claus. Every youngster knew he was busy at the North Pole, and his helpers were scattered about scaring the daylights out of small children.

The mall was alive with Christmas music and lights, and the Salvation Army bells rang in unison, reminding us to love our neighbor as ourselves. I still recall the thrill of having my first Orange Julius, a mouthwatering beverage that I most definitely couldn't find at Truman Lewis' store. A trip to Salisbury took all day, and my sister and I slept much of the way home. The weeks leading up to December 25th, were filled with excitement and anticipation. I noticed a lot of whispering among the adults; I'm sure that the thought of receiving a bunch of new toys was what was most important to most children back then. It is through much older eyes we learn what was really special about Christmas—how as a family we celebrated the birth of Jesus. Every gathering was filled with laughter, fellowship, and delicious food. Most Christmas songs allude to the fact that people are returning home to see their loved ones. Even now, I still have "I'll be home for Christmas" on my playlist. We love to play them while decorating the tree.

Christmas with Mema and Uncle Joe

Every family has unique traditions about the Christmas tree. Some families put up their trees the day after Thanksgiving, while others wait until mid-December. When I was a boy, I remember cruising through the woods with my Pop in search of the perfect size and shape. The trees looked considerably smaller in their natural environment than they did when pulled into the living room. He cut cedar, and even now the scent of it brings back memories of this activity. We used to get a few second glances coming through Lee Mont with a giant cedar tied to the roof of Pop's Volkswagen Beetle. We would stop by Nate Willett's store for a Yoohoo and honey bun. Once the beast had been trimmed and was standing, it was time to decorate. Christmas decorations have evolved quite nicely over the years; I grew up in an era of a cat's best friend, yarn-covered ornaments, and silver tinsel. Anyone who is familiar with them may remember one or two messes that were credited to them. One of my jobs was to unravel the previous year's string lights. Theoretically, they were always neatly rolled and stored for simple unwinding. Once the lights were in a straight line, there was only one thing left to do. Each cord was plugged into the other in a ritual that would make Clark Griswold proud. It never failed that one or two strings would not light. My job was to replace each bulb; decorating a Christmas tree is probably a child's first experience with self-expression. Items made at school found a special spot to hang. We made paper chains and threaded popcorn on long strings, which added a personal touch and a sense of accomplishment for a junior decorator. Wrapping presents is either a blessing or a curse; a true test of a marriage is for a husband and wife to spend an afternoon wrapping Christmas presents. It is usually fairly simple to identify the person who wrapped each gift, from her delicate Origami lesson to his dirty hands' duct tape method. Once wrapped, the gifts found their way under the tree. Of course, these were family gifts; the cornucopia would not arrive until the big guy came on Christmas morning.

The long season of anticipation was soon coming to its climax. The Eastern Shore churches were out in force, singing Christmas carols. The joy of the season is not limited to the very young; everyone, regardless of age, has memories that they hold dear. When I was a child, the morning of Christmas Eve was usually hectic since my mother was in the kitchen most of the day preparing food. My pals and I would call each other to check what was going on at their house, and it was then that I began to second-guess some of my choices on the list to Santa. Wayne Gwaltney had his hopes up, thinking a Zebco 202 was in his future; Carl Ayers had asked for a new erector set--why didn't I think of that? It didn't really matter because the wheels of fate were already in motion. Christmas Eve was a big deal at our house because it was when the extended family exchanged gifts and ate an old country breakfast prepared by Mother. As it got close to bedtime, my sister and I were allowed to open one gift, a teaser for what was to come. I was never particularly skilled in selecting a fun gift to unwrap, but I suppose it didn't really matter because we all need items like T-shirts and underwear.

The last order of business was to leave a snack for the man of the hour, which in our house was the traditional milk and cookies. Bedtime was a theory at best; who ever got a good night's sleep on Christmas Eve? I tossed and turned all night, and my sister and I would sneak into each other's rooms to see if the other had fallen asleep. By 3 am, we were so worn out that we started calling for mom at her bedroom door. When she answered, she would tell us to go back to bed. The admonishment did little to deter us from pleading our case every 30 minutes or so; the techinque usually paid off around 5 o'clock. Mother would climb out of bed with her long chestnut hair all over the place; I don't know about your mother, but mine was not to be messed with until that first cup of coffee was past her lips. We were on the verge of entering the living room when I heard the words that were a dagger to my heart. My sister and I had to wait for our neighbors to arrive before we could examine the haul. These neighbors happened to be our grandparents, and despite moving slower than molasses on Christmas morning, I loved them dearly. Once the sleepy family arrived, it was a time of magic. We were always given the greatest presents, but it wasn't until many years later that I learned about the sacrifices our family made for us. My childhood memories of Santa Claus are ones that I cherish to this day. Blessed with children and grandchildren, I am proud to say that I am still a believer. Peace, love, and joy are always in season.

Chapter 11

Turning the Page

The rich history of the Eastern Shore includes a very unpleasant chapter. In the early days, much of the land was divided into large plantations. Acres of sprawling farmland yielded a variety of crops; the farms were primarily operated with slave labor. Many African American families resided in substandard housing somewhere on the property. There are numerous stories of hope and courage from this trying period.

In the 1780s, a young black man by the name of Harry Hosier was born into slavery. Mr. Hosier gained freedom from slavery and promptly entered the ministry. He preached about hardships, perseverance, and hope. His inspiring messages encouraged Francis Asbury and Thomas Coke to invite the young reverend to preach alongside them to predominantly white congregations. His message of racial equality broke many boundaries and opened the door for many other African Americans to succeed.

In the mid-nineteenth century, the Civil War was raging, and slavery became a hotly debated topic. Thankfully, politicians in Washington, DC began to pass legislation to end the inhumane practice. Many slave owners had begun the process of voluntarily leaving the business, while others would fight to the death to uphold it. The evil was defeated in January 1863. President Abraham Lincoln declared that a document he called the Emancipation Proclamation would free all slaves. However, slavery did not cease on the Eastern Shore or elsewhere. There were local holdouts who refused to obey the order. Many more political debates ensued over the subject of slavery. The Eastern Shore would abolish slavery on April 11, 1864, nearly a year and a half after Lincoln signed the Declaration.

The primary hardship for black citizens is they had been deprived of a good education. There were trailblazers that paved the way for new beginnings. Dr. Thomas Nelson Baker, born as a slave in Eastville in 1860, would use the experience of his humble beginnings to do great things for education. His mother began teaching him the sentences and letters she had learned as a child. She knew that a good education was the key to climbing from poverty. Due to the family's newfound independence, Baker could attend better schools across the Bay. He knew that teaching was his calling. He obtained his Ph.D. in Philosophy from Yale University in

1903, and what remarkable insight and perspective he must have had.

Another outstanding educator was Mary Nottingham Smith. She was born in Northampton County in 1882 and spent the majority of her career working for the Accomack County School system. She was instrumental in persuading teachers to move to rural areas and establish schools. Obtaining textbooks and supplies was difficult enough, but Mary Nottingham Smith's commitment could not be underestimated. Her work in the field of education was memorialized when a new school was built bearing her name. There are countless numbers of people that benefited from her devotion.

I was fortunate enough to grow up in a school system that had long been segregated. As I began researching the history of the Eastern Shore, I recognized that I had a great deal of admiration for the people who battled for racial equality. I didn't realize it at the time, but some of the most important people in my life might not have gotten the opportunities they did if not for those brave souls. One of the most influential teachers in my life was Jack Johnson. He was an art teacher by trade, but he was much more to his students. He prepared us for more than simply painting and pottery; his wisdom provided us with an outstanding head start in life. If nothing else, we learned that a tragic part in our history paved the way for the success of many teachers, nurses, doctors, clergy, and business owners, and we are fortunate to have them. I visited such a business with my grandfather.

Samuel D. Outlaw was a local blacksmith in Onancock. Pop was always fitting his livestock with new adorn-
ments. Mr. Outlaw was a master of his craft, custom
forging objects to his customers' needs. Farmers and
watermen alike were loyal clients. He received his degree
in 1925 and started Onancock's only blacksmith shop in
1927. He worked there until closing in 1991. Mr. Outlaw
was a legend on the Eastern Shore, and his greatest love
was his church, where he served for 46 years as Bethel
AME Church Clerk. His tenure as Sunday School Super-
intendent lasted for 58 years. Samuel D. Outlaw, a prominent businessman, was a founding member of the Eastern
Shore Building and Loan Association. I remember him as
a kind and soft-spoken gentleman that made a huge
impact on this community.

His work has close ties to some of the most historic
events of the twentieth century. The Keller Fair first came
about in the 1880s. In the early days, the Fair was a way
to exhibit farm products. The Turlington Camp Grounds
was the place where many of the items were displayed.
The event was organized by a farmer's society called
Grangers. When the young colts were shown to the
crowd, many of the attendees voiced their displeasure.
The controversy arose as a result of some people's opposi-
tion to horse racing. The Grangers went to work looking
for nearby land to pursue a new location. They were
successful in their endeavors, and they built what was
known as "Grange Hall." They immediately went to work
to construct a half-mile race track. James E. Mears chroni-

cled many of these events in his writings. The new establishment was called the "Eastern Shore Agricultural Fair", and it was here that "Keller Fair" was born. According to Mears, a large grandstand was constructed for housing the spectators. As the fair's appeal spread to Shore residents, new attractions were added; this was an incredible venue for vendors to display their products. Back then, word-of-mouth was the only form of advertising. This prompted chefs, bakers, and canners to bring their best items to sample.

The popularity of the fair and all the festivities inspired an entirely new sense of fashion. Those attending the horse races were dressed with impeccable style. The ladies were elegant and charming from head to toe, while men looked dapper in their new suits, top hats, and gold cufflinks. In Keller, Virginia, a new trend in horse racing apparel emerged. In the summer, the Eastern Shore sun is relentless, and gnats may ruin a pleasant day. To combat both, the ladies wore large brim hats adorned with anything rumored to repel an insect. This tradition would spread across the sport. You may have seen such a hat at the Kentucky Derby. There were several categories for horse racing on the Shore because it was so popular. One of the most popular was the "Sulky" races. This was a wooden cart on wheels attached to the back of the horse. Instead of riding horseback, the jockey was in the cart, encouraging the animal to run faster. The Keller Fair flourished throughout the decades, and Samuel Outlaw did some of his best work there. Anyone that has ever raised horses knows the importance of a qualified black-smith. Many of the horseshoes were hammered out and custom fitted in a small shop in Onancock, Virginia. Samuel Outlaw's professionalism and innovation impacted a whole generation. The Keller Fair and Mr. Outlaw were both Class Acts, leaving a legacy of smiles and satisfaction in their wake.

Chapter 12

A Ferry Tale

Traveling on the Eastern Shore was not always simple. For example, a day trip across the bay was not very practical. In the 1930s, a ferry system was put in place to connect travelers from Virginia Beach to Cape Charles. In those days, ferries were designed to transport passengers. The trip across the mouth of Chesapeake Bay was occasionally thrilling, as the weather on the water changed with the wind and tides. The ferries were put through their paces by the relentless bayside chop. The Little Creek/Cape Charles fleet has traditionally been praised for its safety record. The ferries' schedules were frequently coordinated with the Pennsylvania Rail Road Company; rail was still a popular means of transportation in the early twentieth century—it seemed so modern and convenient at the time. More technology was introduced in the 1940s, and the ferry system quickly transformed from being merely a passenger carrier to a fleet that could also transport vehicles. This marked the beginning of the decline in traveling by railroad. Drivers were finding independence as they drove their own vehicles up and down the coast. The terminal locations changed over the years. In the late 1940s, the Eastern Shore terminal moved from Cape Charles to Kiptopeake. Time and technology weighed heavily on the future of the Ferry system, and engineers and dreamers had bold ideas about a more efficient method of travel back and forth across the Chesapeake Bay. The blueprints became a reality in 1964 when the 17.6-mile span of bridge and tunnel was completed, a revolutionary marvel at the time. The Chesapeake Bay Bridge Tunnel was about to change life on the Eastern Shore; there would be no need to wait in line or adhere to a schedule. This contemporary innovation was a dagger to the heart of the long-admired ferry industry; there is always some sadness associated with losing things in the name of progress; Ferries were simply a part of life in the early twentieth century. Many people on the Eastern Shore and beyond recall those moments with joy. Teresa Pruitt tells her experience onboard the Pocahontas for a day trip to Norfolk to do some back-to-school shopping. Many families depended on the ferry to keep in touch with loved ones. Anne Rolander remembers running around the deck as a child; her father's family lived in Norfolk, making the Rolanders frequent passengers. I can only imagine the wonder of boarding these floating cities through the eyes of a child. Anne spoke of the sounds and scents; the salt air is crisp and fresh, and every Shoreborn soul knows what that marsh mud smell means to them.

The ferries were massive and designed to handle tons of cargo. An amazing thought of loading automobiles and large trucks onto a boat. Although most trips were fairly uneventful, the bay is not always kind; some passengers recall some rocking and rolling. After all, this is where the Atlantic Ocean and the Chesapeake Bay collide. I can close my eyes and envision the men looking dapper in a fedora and tailored suits -- these were gentlemen with honor and class. Many of them had served their country in some branch of the military. The ladies were equally stunning; their wardrobes were hand-picked, and they were adorned with lovely jewelry and the latest hairstyle of that period.

People depended on the service of the ferry to be able to attend weddings, birthday parties, and holiday visits. No one ever thought of the ferry as an inconvenience; on the contrary, everyone was grateful for the service and the entire crew who made it possible. The nostalgia associated with the ferry and railroad system is one of the most fascinating aspects of our unique Eastern Shore history. Carlton "Sonny" Shrieves worked as a machinist for the Pennsylvania Railroad Company, and his son Carl Shrieves remembers living next to the Little Creek ferry terminal. He thinks about the wonderful relationship he and his father had with the railroad and ferry families; they made many trips to Cape Charles to visit family. Ralph Crumb was the Captain of the Pocahontas at the time, and like many passengers, Mr. Shrieves preferred to board the majestic Princess Anne.

In those days, Cape Charles was in high gear; the railroad and the busy port had turned the area into a boomtown as early as the late 1800s. By the turn of the century, Cape Charles was installing modern conveniences, such as electricity and paved roads, which were previously exclusive to big cities. The history surrounding the rise of Cape Charles is fascinating and it all began with our beloved railroads. In the 1870s, the railroad only came as far south as Pocomoke City, Maryland. William L. Scott was a Pennsylvania politician with ties to the railroad industry. Mr. Scott had the vision to extend the rails all the way down to Virginia's Eastern Shore. His idea was to marry the rail system with a barge company to allow passengers and valuable goods to reach the Norfolk area. Many people were skeptical of his ideas, and Scott didn't make much progress with them. However, things turned around for him when he teamed up with a young traffic engineer employed by the Pennsylvania Railroad Company. Alexander Cassatt believed that Mr. Scott's vision could someday become a reality, so he left his position, and the two men set to go to work on the massive undertaking.

The first step was to secure land on the Eastern Shore's southern tip. The area had to be suitable for rail and a busy port to meet near the mouth of the Chesapeake Bay. Cassatt wanted to survey the route the new section of rails would be laid, so he mounted up on horseback and headed south from Pocomoke. Cassatt was laying out a grid on where he thought the rail would meet the least resistance as he traveled. Farmland and forests with towering pine and oak trees made up most of the landscape; railroads in the barren wild west seldom encountered such obstacles. Cassatt continued south down the center of the Eastern Shore, undaunted by the obstructions. He relied on the hospitality of local families to rest up for a while; practically every farm on the Shore in those days could easily accommodate the needs of a horse and a tired traveler dusty from the trail. Cassatt frequently remarked on how well he was treated throughout his travels. As he made his way south in 1883, his partner William L. Scott was in the process of closing the deal on a large portion of land needed to complete the process. The Tazwell family owned almost 2,500 acres of land that was included in the purchase, which was made up of three plantations. The men sectioned out approximately 140 acres for both residential and business usage; this was the humble beginning of the town of Cape Charles. In 1884, the area was mapped out into seven avenues traveling east to west, and it was decided that these avenues would be named after prominent citizens in the state. The streets that would run north to south were to be named after various fruits. With the deal for bringing the rails south down the Eastern Shore secured , Cape Charles was on its way to becoming one of the most popular destinations on the east coast for good jobs and modern housing. A trip that used to take weeks was reduced to days and, later, hours. Folks could now travel by rail from New York to Cape Charles and by boat across the bay. This also meant that the precious commodities grown on the Shore could be transported to higher markets, allowing many families to climb out of decades of poverty and even make some very wealthy. In the early days of construction, Cape Charles could have dozens of houses being built at the same time; some are sprawling structures with wraparound porches, while beachfront residences were occasionally three stories. Large dormer windows were installed, providing residents and guests with a grand view of the busy port and the majestic sunsets over the Chesapeake Bay. The homes were situated near pristine sandy beaches and shallow, swimmable waters. I can close my eyes and see myself sitting on one of those front porches, watching the town come to life. It must have been an exciting period for those who lived it. As the nineteenth century faded away, businesses that had recently installed hitching posts and water troughs had to make way for automobiles. Another tradition, the use of horses and buggies, was set to be replaced by technology as Norfolk began mass-producing cars. Cassatt and Scott had made it possible to ship them to northern markets up and down the east coast. Cape Charles remains an inspiring story about innovation, perseverance, and the basic principles of capitalism.

The railroad had an immeasurable social and

economic impact on the Eastern Shore. Towns sprang up all along the route plotted out by Mr. Cassatt, and the rails changed how business was done. For centuries, farmers depended on wagons and horses to transport their crops to market. Shipping was mainly done on the Chesapeake Bay, and anything being transported off the Shore was taken on a slow ride to the nearest port. The challenge was to keep perishable items fresh by the time they reached their destination. With the arrival of the railroads, everything would change. The majority of larger towns had depot stations, and routine stops were scheduled to load passengers as well as cargo.

Almost overnight, the economic wave was felt over the Delmarva Peninsula and the whole east coast. With residents earning more money, homes were built at a blistering pace, and new enterprises began forming and flourishing. For the Eastern Shore, the whine of that train's whistle symbolized modern technology and prosperity. Victorian and Cape Cod-style residences began to replace smaller wooden houses constructed with whatever materials were available at the time. Pride was evident in every structure created in the early days, as shown by the ornate architecture and detail placed in each home built. No house on the Eastern Shore was more majestic than our churches. Most of them are adorned with towering steeples and stained glass. The boards were hand cut from lumber which is still solid today. Inside the attics of many of our historic homes, you will find boards that still have bark and some that have sap coming from them even after 100 years. The builders even used sea shells in some of the mortar mixtures in the foundation.

There is one Eastern Shore value that every citizen believes in: waste not, want not. People know how to make use of everything around them, and all of this progress can be credited to the railroad.

In the early days, building supplies could take weeks or months to arrive. With the rails, you could have whatever you needed to complete a job with a few days' notice. Passenger cars with plush seats replaced old rickety wagons. Much more comfortable than an old squeaky seat staring at a mule's rear end on a week-long trip up north. Railroad towns like Hallwood were revolutionary in the way farmers marketed their crops. In 1903, John W. Taylor built a canning facility there, which was a fairly progressive idea for a small town at the time. Instead of being shipped to a large city, The John W. Taylor packing company was place to have the local gold canned and labeled. Thanks to Mr. Taylor's vision, fresh harvests like tomatoes and sweet potatoes were able to travel from the field to the grocery store. Many Shore residents found work at the factory, which marked the beginning of families earning two incomes. Rolling smoke south down the tracks, villages like Bloxom were in high gear. All these towns had their own general stores and were self-sustaining for the most part.

Another boom town was Parksley, which also had a

large factory. R & G Shirt Factory specialized in the production of dresses and other popular clothing. One of the largest barrel manufacturing operations was located nearby, and the majority of the items were stored in barrels for shipping. Dunne Avenue and Bennett Street evolved as the town's business centers. Parksley, like most of our towns, had room for more than one church. Parksley, a beautiful Hamlet to this day, was home to some of the most spectacular residences on the east coast. My hometown of Greenbush is located on the rail just south of Parksley. I can still hear the engineer's lone whistle signaling his arrival at each intersection.

There isn't a kid anywhere that wasn't fascinated by a Choo Choo train. As the coal smoke billowed from the stack, the next stop was Tasley, which was a bustling economic hub back then. Many businesses thrived in the centrally located village. The feed mill was one of the largest establishments. The Peninsula Milling and Feed Company catered to the needs of all livestock owners. In the old days, it was rare to find a family not tending to chickens and other livestock. Life on the Eastern Shore has endured for many generations due to that sense of independence. Mills were the very essence of life on the Shore. The Indians made their own mills out of large stones, and grain was ground into flour and used in almost all recipes in some way or another. Tasley was previously known as Accomac Station, and the town's success was primarily dependent on the busy rail system. Produce was delivered there before being transported to Onancock, where large steamships were waiting. The goods were shipped to Baltimore and then distributed to other markets. Route 13, the Shore's major highway, went through the center of Tasley which made it a popular stop for those traveling by automobile. The town can lay claim to Accomack County's first paved road, electric power facility, and Volunteer Fire Company. In Tasley, you could find anything you needed. Several restaurants stayed packed with patrons. In the Shore's economic boom, car and tractor dealerships prospered as customers flocked to the town. Four businesses could be found close to one another, and Copes Ice Plant has been a staple of Tasley for decades. There, Mr. Leon would become known as a Shore legend and earn the nickname "Ice Man". Tasley's sawmills were churning out lumber all day, and the demand for new houses kept the mills running at full capacity. Living on the Shore at that time was another exciting experience. Nowadays, the town is mostly ghostly quiet, with the exception of the Tasley Volunteer Fire Department, which is still active in the community. Every time I ride through this small town, I imagine how it may have appeared in the past.

Onley was the train's next stop. The name "Cross-roads" came from the fact that Onley had roads connecting it to Wachapreague, Onancock, and nearby Accomac. As the town grew, the name Onley was given to it, and its central location made it an ideal location for auctions. Farmers would bring potatoes, strawberries, and grain into the large area near the train depot. Brokers representing prospective buyers would haggle about the price they were willing to pay. The markets were determined by setting a standard for how much similar things might bring in other places. Many people believe that the Eastern Shore is falling behind other places; yet, the Shore has blazed a new trail for many future entrepreneurs. Long gone were the days of a farmer and his family out beside the road trying to sell the harvest. Onley was another of the towns that seemingly came together overnight. East and West Main Streets are on opposite sides of the railroad tracks, and there are beautiful homes on both sides. The churches in Onley exhibit the same attention to detail and stunning design as others built during that historical period. Onley has faced its share of difficulties; unfortunately, the entire business district was destroyed by a massive fire many decades ago. Although the railroad has long since disappeared, those who were there remember the scent of those strawberries clearly.

The next stop was Melfa. It is true that the rails inspired much growth and paved the way for new businesses. Long before the rails were laid, the Eastern Shore had thriving communities. Thomas Walker was the proprietor of a prosperous hat factory in the 1700s that was located in Melfa. It was known for producing colonial-style hats, which were quite fashionable at the time. The factory has since faded into the obscurity of Eastern Shore history. That was not the last time Mr. Walker's name would adorn a local business. After a couple hundred years, the Downing family acquired the land where the hat factory formerly stood. They were in a completely different line of work; local families depended on dairy farms for milk, butter, and cheese. The Downings maintained a profitable bottling and delivery business named: "Walker Folly Farms" in honor of Thomas Walker.

Jim Brown and his wife handled day-to-day operations, and they kept two delivery trucks to keep families stocked up. In the good old days, there were several dairy farms in operation. Green Hill serviced Accomack County's northernmost portion, while Nelson was busy in the Onancock area. Walkers Folly farms served clientele on the central Shore; the largest dairy farm at the time was near Nassawadox, which was known as Mapleton. Mr. Teagle Whitehead was the man in charge of the operations. The milkman is remembered with affection by many Shore residents. They frequented most households twice a week, making them extended family. A bit south was an interesting town named Keller. Residents on the outskirts of civilization were eager to move into town, which had several stores in operation. Keller and neighboring towns were home to railroad mills that made the ties that held the tracks together. The development of churches in towns was another factor in people moving there. Painter was among the towns seeing rapid growth. The local church, Painter-Garrison's United Methodist Church, was established in 1784, and at the time of its founding, it had a capacity congregation. The Shore was built on dreams and faith. Belle Haven and Exmore were two more bustling communities. The Eastern Shore, like many other densely populated areas, was beginning to reap the benefits of the Industrial Revolution. Factories that were previously reserved for major cities found a home on the rural Eastern Shore. The reason for this was the abundance of eager people looking for full-time employment. Coca-Cola was one of the first national brands to set up shop in Exmore Virginia, operating a bottling facility, warehouse, and distribution operation. The town prospered like never before, and other businesses were doing just as well.

Another sizable packaging facility in Exmore was Dulany's. Many families on the Eastern Shore can recall either working there or having a family member who did. My grandmother was employed there for a period of time. Dulany's was ahead of their time since they could package and keep perishable foods due to their ability to freeze. This earned them the nickname the "Freezer Plant" by the locals. Dulany's even ran a bus service to and from the plant to help folks get to work. Once only a dream, many Eastern Shore families could now afford things like automobiles and televisions. Exmore shares the familiar theme of all the other railroad communities. Soon, Exmore and Belle Haven would be home to restaurants, merchants, car dealerships, and more. I imagine similar stories can be found along any railroad communities of that era.

If you wish to go even further back in time, you can visit Northhampton County's Crown Jewel, Eastville.

They take pride in having the nation's oldest continuous court records. Eastville established itself as Northampton's County Seat in 1680 and built its first courthouse in 1731. Some 40 years later, on the courthouse steps in 1776, a small document was read aloud, and the community heard the Declaration of Independence for the first time. The history of Eastville and the surrounding districts of Machipongo, Cheriton, and Cape Charles is fascinating. Many of the people who shaped an early nation had ties to Northampton County. The county is known for having some of the best soil for growing crops on the east coast. The area's primary source of income comes from acres of sprawling farmland; this is how generations of Shore farmers made a living. When the name "Arlington Plantation" was chosen for the national cemetery, it drew attention across the country. Northampton, like most of the Shore, has a line of barrier islands along its seaside coast. Some of these areas were first occupied by Indians, and Hog Island was originally known as Machipongo Island. This translates to "fine dust and flies" in the language of the Natives. Some of the islands were inhabited until storms wreaked havoc and the mighty Atlantic Ocean began to reclaim the beaches. In comparison to other nearby islands, Rogue, Cobb, Little Cobb, and Wreck Islands are somewhat distant from the mainland. They undoubtedly spared the lower Shore from a battery of vicious storms. Many love to venture out to the barrier islands for beach combing and fishing. The remaining lower Shore seaside paradises include Ship

Shoal, Godwin, Myrtle, Mink, and Smith Islands. A nice sight for the early tourists who had been on a ship for a month. No matter how fine the dust is between your toes or where you swat a horsefly, one thing is constant: Once the Eastern Shore has worked her magic on your soul, you'll never be able to shake it from your heart.

Chapter 13

Round Up

E very Eastern Shore kid remembers waking up to the sound of cicadas on a hot July morning. In the good old days, air conditioning was considered a luxury. Most people just left the windows up and circulated the hot air with an old metal fan. There was always the hope that a good old-fashioned thunderstorm might roll up the Chesapeake Bay and cool things down. My sister and I didn't usually have a hard time falling asleep. We would spend our nights in the backyard catching lightning bugs after long days of fun in the sun. So much fun and so many memories were created with a simple mason jar with a few holes poked in the lid. Some summer mornings were much more significant than others. I remember counting down the days to the last Wednesday in July. From the eyes of a child, the Eastern Shore tradition of Pony Penning was quite the adventure. Judging by the number of adults in attendance, it is safe to say everyone gets caught up in the magic. The two-day event, which consists of the pony swim and auction, is the largest fundraiser for the Chincoteague Volunteer Fire Department. The event has a rich history attached to it. For generations, people have debated how the herd got on Assateague. Some contend that the ponies were brought to the island sometime in the 17th century. Like most subjects with no eyewitnesses, the door is wide open for all sorts of theories. Many believe that the herd arrived at the beach in a much more dramatic fashion. The Atlantic coast has always been a popular shipping route, dating back to the 16th century. According to legend, a Spanish galleon filled with gold and livestock sunk in the waters off Assateague Island. Numerous animals reportedly survived the event and made their way to the sands of Assateague Beach. With acres to roam and a lot of food, the herd is believed to have survived and grown despite the odds. One truth that cannot be disputed is that the wild ponies have been present for as long as anyone recalls. Long before there was a fire department, some of the ponies were claimed and brought back to local farms. Sheep were also abundant on the island at the time, so they were rounded up and relocated as well. These appear to be the humble beginnings of what has since become known around the globe as Pony Penning. While the sheep population eventually faded into the past the pony population continued to thrive and reproduce. The early twentieth century was a dreadful time for Chincoteague Island, as a couple of devastating fires left the town struggling to rebuild. In 1922, the Causeway connecting Chincoteague to the mainland was near completion. To protect the island, the residents realized they needed their own fire department. This marked the start of the modern era of Pony Penning. In 1924, it was decided that some of the herd would be sold to help offset the costs of the new fire equipment. Even then, a foal might sell for $25 to $50. The fire department became the official owners and keepers of the wild Assateague Ponies.

Training a Chincoteague Pony

In the 1920s, crowds of over 25,000 people gathered to witness the exciting event. The swim has been an annual favorite ever since. Meanwhile, back in the 70s, it was my turn to watch for the first time. Mom was making sandwiches for a picnic basket, and Pop was loading his truck with those fold-up chairs with all the different colors woven together. We were waiting for my Uncle Hub to arrive from Baltimore. He would stay with his sister, my Aunt Ida. Back then, many events on the Shore involved the entire family. I remember the adults making plans to eat dinner at Wright's Restaurant. I loved that place and the view despite the fact that I had to travel to Bill Hickman's store to get fitted for a new sports jacket. I never quite knew what those crazy elbow pads were all about. My sister Valerie and I were no strangers to Chincoteague ponies as children, thanks to my grandfather. The experience never seemed to get old.

Every boy grew up watching Westerns on television. These were real horses and cowboys from the Eastern Shore, not your typical trail-riding cowboy. These guys earned the honorable nickname of "Salt Water Cowboys." These are proud members of the fire department that mount up to help gather the herd. I remember Pop stopping to talk to everyone as we arrived on the island. He knew all the Saltwater Cowboys, including Jack Brittingham, John Wesley Bloxom, and David Savage. All these men were on horseback and ready to ride. Their horses were well-groomed and well-mannered. They had to be because many of the activities take place within feet of the spectators. As we moved closer to the channel, Harry Stanley Thornton, Billy, and Delmas Taylor were on horseback, monitoring the tide. Depending on the tide, the ponies will swim across the Assateague Channel. Slack tide, a brief period when the water is not moving, is the best time for the ponies to swim. When the time is right, the Saltwater Cowboys guide the ponies into the water and stay with them until the last one has safely made the crossing. Pop used to lift me up on his shoulders to get a better view. Hanging around in the marsh in the middle of summer is not for the faint of heart. Gnats, mosquitoes, and horseflies are among the legion of onlookers; this is all part of the charm of such an event. Once the ponies are safely on the Chincoteague side, they are escorted down Ridge Road to the Carnival Grounds. The streets are lined with locals and tourists, creating a parade atmosphere. The ponies are then given the opportunity to rest and receive a checkup from a local veterinarian. Many of the herd will be returned to graze the marshes of Assateague. The events on Wednesday will now come to an end, and Thursday will bring in a new crowd. In keeping with tradition, some of the ponies will be auctioned off. The days of a $50 foal are long gone. As the event gains popularity, the price of a Chincoteague Pony reflects the commitment required to maintain a healthy herd. The swim and auction signal the beginning of the much-anticipated Chincoteague Carnival. The fire department and numerous volunteers work together to put on the family-friendly event. Clam Fritters, Hamburgers, Hotdogs, and Pizza are all on the menu, along with a nice sweet funnel cake and a cold beverage to wash it all down. The special thing about Chincoteague's carnival is the number of visitors that have been able to enjoy it. The popularity of Pony Penning has reached global attention. Celebrities and VIPs from all over the world have traveled thousands of miles to attend the festivities. For a Shoreborn kid, this was just another cool party in my own backyard.

My sister and I in the pony cart

The people of Chincoteague and Assateague are survivors. One of the most powerful noreasters ever recorded ravaged the islands in 1962. The month was March, and the violent storm will be remembered for the day it arrived, Ash Wednesday. The locals have braved many storms over the decades. Many decided to ride out the storm as they had done in the past. One factor that they didn't account for was the catastrophic flooding that accompanied the storm surge. Cars were washed into the rising salty waters, and escape via the causeway was impossible. Residents of two-story homes retreated to the second floor with the hope that the rising waters would soon recede. There was no choice but to wait for rescue for those who remained on the island. Both the Coast Guard and the National Guard were deployed. Many of the town's heroes were boat-owning Chincoteague citizens, who helped shocked locals to higher ground without any professional rescue training. Jan Clark's Aunt Etta lived on Main Street, and Jan recalls a somber conversation as residents witnessed caskets floating in the streets. At the time, Glenda Barnes Lovelady was only 8 years old. She remembers standing in line to be evacuated by helicopter to the mainland. Large boats were resting in backyards in the days after the storm, which had left Chincoteague looking like a wasteland. Additionally, numerous first-story windows had been broken by the storm's powerful waves. The island's restoration took months, if not years. There is one thing that the Ash Wednesday storm couldn't wash away: the resilience of the Chincoteague Community. Much like the ponies that survived the odds all those centuries ago, Chincoteague and Assateague Islands are thriving today.

Chapter 14

Living "The Dream"

The 1950s were considered by many as the birth of the modern era. Throughout this decade, the presidents were Harry S. Truman and Dwight D. Eisenhower. They were both beneficiaries of a manufacturing boom in the United States. Surplus from the war was repurposed into items that the average family could utilize, and new technology was in place to replace things like the wringer washing machine. Larger and more efficient models were making their way into the ordinary home. The old mechanical lawnmowers began collecting dust in the garage corner. Newer models fitted with internal combustion engines could cut work time in half. Every day, more people were using the radio and television, and Buddy Holly and the Big Bopper were becoming more well-known in the music scene. Humphrey Bogart, Marlon Brando, and Jimmy Stewart were considered darlings of the Silver Screen. The cars were stylish and fast, and the Chevrolet BelAir was as American as apple pie—what an awesome time to be a teenager. Meanwhile, back on the Eastern Shore, it's Saturday night. Tim Prettyman and the other cool cats are set to meet up at Exmore's Lloyds drugstore. When they arrived, Bobby Thomas and Arthur Webb were already waiting. Back in the day, many local establishments had a soda fountain, and patrons loved a chocolate zip while socializing and celebrating their youth. Long-handled dispensers were pulled down to fill frosty glasses with tasty beverages. This earned the clerk the not-so-flattering nickname of "Soda Jerk". Every town had a place like this for people to mingle; they were fantastic places for young people to hang out in safety and have a good time. If you were in Cape Charles, you may run upon Betty Lou Marshall Johnson enjoying a chocolate nut Sundae at Griff's. She was waiting for Jean Hunt Steffens and Gwen Alter to arrive so they could make some after-school plans. Patricia Nock claimed that the Cherry Bon Bons at Savage's drugstore down the street was the best on the Shore.

In the 1950s, there were joyful events called Sock Hops. Faye Collins recalls dancing the night away at Franktown United Methodist Church. Parents didn't have to be worried since there was always supervision; everything you did that evening made it home before you did. On the Shore, there has always been a strong sense of community and family. Manners were taught, and youth and adults shared mutual respect. Elizabeth Taylor recalls working at the Candlelight at the time. Local kids were treated as if they were your own, and they were well cared for. Pete Hopkins and the boys were down around Onancock Way, where Cherry Smashes cost 6 cents a pop and were a treat. Comic books were also very popular in that era. Many of the other kids were at Forks Grill and Wise's drugstore. Parksley was home to Pep Phillips' place which served as a one-stop shop for refreshments and sporting goods. Carter Davis recalls the Pony Ranch in Pocomoke and Claude Linton's on Saxis. Many of these places paved the way for the Crown Jewel of family entertainment. In 1955, a young man named Jimmy Justice and his wife Mary Lou had a dream in the small town of Wattsville. The Justices believed that if they constructed a building large enough to house a skating rink, people would come for miles to have some good old-fashioned family fun. To make it even better, the couple envisioned a game room and a small restaurant. They succeeded in creating a spot known as "The Dream." In retrospect, we know this establishment was a part of Pop Culture for decades. There isn't a person on the Shore who can't share a memory of when they were open. Many first dates took place on this hallowed ground, and some of them went on to marry and have children. This wasn't your ordinary run-of-the-mill business, the Justices were able to capture a mood. There were many carefree, joyful days spent in laughter. The unique aspect is that many of the parents who enjoyed skating there now had children old enough to attend. Throughout the 1960s, 1970s, and 1980s, the business grew to include a bus service that would pick you up at the door and return you to your destination at a designated time. You'd be mistaken if you thought Mr. Jimmy hired a bus driver; that position was far too important for him to entrust someone else. You guessed it—Jimmy Justice was behind the wheel of the transport bus. He was strict as well as kind, and as long as you respected him and Mary Lou, you were in his good graces. If you crossed that line, he quickly made you aware.

The Dream's bus schedule

"The Dream" was the first place I saw a neon sign. Walking through the front door was an experience in and of itself, with the sound of billiard balls and guys telling jokes. The aroma of fried onions and cheeseburgers cooking on a flat grill. The red stools were packed with happy customers, and I had a Cherry Coke in my future. There was always an age gap between patrons, but it didn't seem to matter because there was something for everyone. I recall making my way across the game room to the door leading to the skating rink, which was only a few steps down into a hallway. This was an obstacle that gave me a fit trying to negotiate in roller skates. The corridor was lined with Polaroid photos, some of which were recent and some of which were black and white. There was one thing they all had in common: everyone was smiling. As I made my way to the hardwood floor, the sound of the latest tunes was on the loudspeakers. There was a certain art form that proficient skaters displayed. The crossing of the skates and a modest 360 were simply trademarks of the regulars. The owner himself, Jimmy Justice, was among the best skaters I've ever seen. He wore so many hats that the kids thought of him as Superman, and he was undoubtedly a father figure to many more people than he realized. Jimmy oversaw the skating and also worked the microphone. He would call for "Couples Skate". This was the cue for the shy boy to come up and take the hand of a young lady for a spin around the rink. There's nothing like watching all the couples sing along to Endless Love while struggling to stand with your wheels on.

There were many different commands while skating, and I'm sure you remember your favorite. Then there came a shout over the speakers that said, "How low can you go?" This was in preparation for the very popular Limbo. The vertical balance of a person would be tested by a series of horizontal obstacles; for some reason, the tallest folks always seemed to win. During the special skating events, several of us would go back up those troublesome steps. The Juke Box was a thrill all to itself; for a quarter, you could listen to any tune you wanted. Time flew by at the Dream Roller Rink. Four hours on a Saturday afternoon passed by, and we were back on the bus to Four Corners. Many of us learned much more than skating and socializing. The Dream was a gateway from adolescence to adulthood. Those fortunate enough to experience these special times will cherish the memories for a lifetime.

Memory Lane

Coming of age is a special time in everyone's life, and young adults on the Eastern Shore were out and about embracing their freedom. In the good old days, dances with live bands were playing at many different venues. The Legion Hall was a popular spot to shake a leg. Many partygoers made their rounds until they found the right crowd and music genres for them. In places like Daddy Wise and Kinsey's Seaside Club, the blues and jazz were popular. Folks claim that if you were lucky enough to be there on the right nights, you might catch a live performance by some music legends. Artists like James Brown and Fats Domino frequently traveled through our area on their way to shows in New Jersey and New York—what a thrill that must have been. The Onancock Armory was packed almost every evening. Local bands like Full Sail delighted the audience with southern rock hits. Many couples started their road to matrimony by first meeting at these famous spots. Twin Towers in Pocomoke even had lodging for those that enjoyed too much of the nightlife. The Trawler was a very popular spot for the people in the Exmore area. The best part about hanging out there and at The Island House in Wachapreague was the incredible seafood on the menu. The Pony Pines and Captain Fish's were favorites among Chincoteague residents. These names certainly bring back nostalgic feelings for many people. Hopefully, no one will be reminded of a well-deserved hangover.

Chapter 15

Shoreborn Memoir

I have been blessed to grow up Shoreborn. I have never lived anywhere else, and quite frankly, I don't believe that I could. Our way of life is embedded in my heart and seared into my soul. My family means everything to me. My beautiful wife, Linda, and amazing daughter, Kamryn, and I still reside in the house my grandfather built in Greenbush. Our son, Matthew, lives in Onancock with our two grandchildren, Paige and Carter. I am thankful to still have my mother, and I often sit with her in her childhood home. She tells me stories about days gone by. The memories and recollections of her generation are the best records of the past. The Santa Claus suit that my pop, Ralph Melson, used to thrill youngsters rests comfortably in my attic. As I get older my time is spent with far less adventure. I enjoy volunteering on community projects with the Onancock Elks Lodge. It is there that I have witnessed the heart of a generous Eastern Shore, working with Wayde Fowler on fundraisers are cherished memories. Some days I sit back and enjoy a warm summer breeze. A glass of sweet tea and the smell of honeysuckle still makes me smile. This is when I take stock of all the blessings in my life. Friendships and relationships enjoyed for a lifetime. Mike, Scotty and I still like to ride down to Hunting Creek and go fishing and crabbing with William and the guys. Ben Justis was always on his family dock with a kind word and a joke to tell. I have had the same neighbors for over 50 years. The Johnson family is synonymous with the town of Greenbush. I am just proud to call them my friends. Many other aspects of my youth have changed dramatically. Wal Mart and Food Lion have replaced the mom and pop stores. We are thankful for the memories. I spend much of my time dusting off old photographs, they are windows into the past. Each picture tells a unique story, whether it's a 1920s wedding or a 1960s graduation. One thing ties them all together: they depicted something very important in a family's life. I try and preserve as many as possible and reunite them with relatives whenever I can. Many of the businesses that we once celebrated have faded into the past. Recently, I sat in my car in the old Copes Ice Plant parking lot. Places like these allow me to reminisce and collect my thoughts. The first thing I noticed when I rolled down my window was how quiet it was. The deafening silence replaced Leon hollering for you to raise your tailgate as the ice filled the truck bed. The Farmex parking lot is now filled with weeds instead of delivery trucks. I closed my eyes and listened for the sound of a sawmill ripping some long pine boards. I thought I heard them, along with the whistle of the afternoon train, but it was all in my imagination. By this time of day, the feed mill should be hopping with farmers loading up bags of corn. The wagons should be lined up along the tracks, loading and unloading goods and passengers—again, silence. I was getting hungry when I came to the realization all the restaurants were closed. I yearn for the days when I could slip down and shoot the breeze with Otho Lewis. A cloth bologna sandwich sounds amazing about now. I don't say these words to depress you; rather, they are meant to remind everyone of our beloved past. It is up to us to salvage the stories and honor the rich Eastern Shore heritage. The railroad, which was once a lifeline to our prosperity, was taken away rail by rail and board by board. It's difficult to watch if you truly appreciate how much blood and sweat it took to build. The sacrifice railroad families made was selfless and heroic, and you can imagine how valuable a penny smashed on the tracks is today. I am forever an optimist and advocate for the Eastern Shore, our beautiful islands, and the entire Delmarva Peninsula. I would love to ride by the churchyard and see three dozen bicycles and their riders playing baseball beneath a Shoreborn sky. I pray for the day that I can take my grandchildren, Paige and Carter, down to Wachapreague to watch the legendary fleet return to port. We owe an enormous debt of gratitude to every single soul that paved the way to paradise. It is my sincere hope that we someday return to the traditions we all love and cherish. I will continue to experience them every day, if only in my Shoreborn mind.

Acknowledgments

Thanks for the inspiration of the entire Shoreborn family. Without you, this project would not be possible. Dr. John Robertson paved the way to preserving Eastern Shore history. He was at the cutting edge of photography in the early days. Kirk Mariner, Curtis Badger, and Dennis Custis were a huge influence on this project. My heart beats for the members of the Eastern Shore and I am forever grateful for the stories shared and memories made.

About the Author

Barry Mears is a visionary and devoted Shoreborn citizen. Growing up on the Shore taught him about core values such as family, faith, and the power of community. He is committed to spreading the history of the Eastern Shore as well as bringing together those who have since moved away. In his book, "Living Shoreborn" he tells a true story about his childhood, as well as the antiquity of the Eastern Shore of Virginia.

Made in the USA
Columbia, SC
24 March 2025

55631169R00074